Agile and Scrum

*Unlock the Power of Agile Project
Management, Lean Thinking, the Kanban
Process, and Scrum*

Contents

Part 1: Agile

What You Need to Know About Agile Project Management, the Kanban Process, Lean Thinking, and Scrum

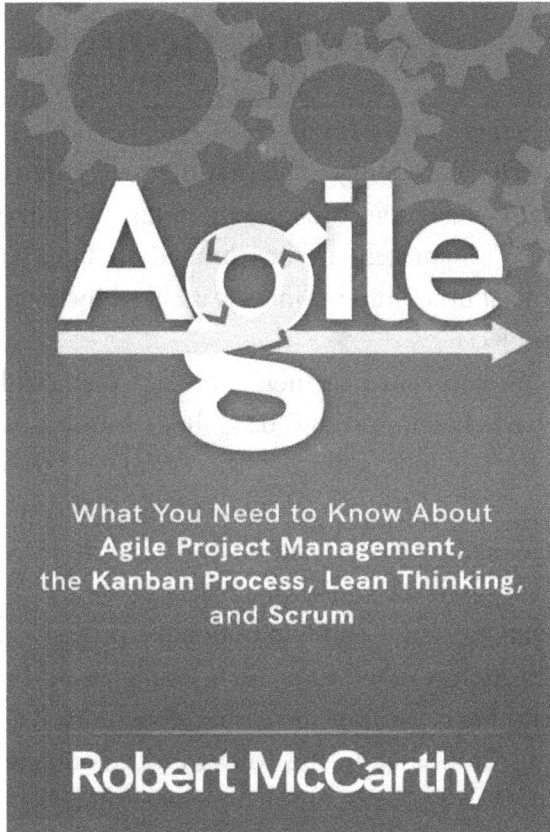

Introduction

Project management is the practice of guiding projects from their start to end while successfully achieving the project goals. Historical evidence suggests that project management has been in existence for centuries. Project management was limited to large and complex projects for a long time until businesses realized the need for smaller and simpler projects.

Different project management tools, methodologies, and frameworks have been introduced to help businesses and teams develop products and services successfully. However, every methodology, tool, and framework has its pros and cons. Traditional project management methodologies that were practiced until the 21st century were largely linear and sequential.

The limitations of such traditional project management methodologies often resulted in projects being late and costing more than estimated. There was an increasing demand for a new project management methodology in the software development industry to help teams deliver projects on time while adjusting to changing requirements of customers instead of avoiding them.

In February 2001, seventeen software development practitioners and experts gathered at a ski resort in Utah. The group would later go on to be known as The Agile Alliance. The outcome of the gathering was the introduction of the Agile Manifesto. This introduced four values and twelve principles that described a new project management methodology aimed at solving the challenges faced by the software development industry at the time.

Many software development companies embraced the core values and guiding principles. Smaller teams working on shorter development cycles, while regularly receiving feedback from customers, enabled projects to be more open toward change instead of avoiding it. Self-organizing and cross-functional teams made projects easier to manage, while team members took ownership of their increased productivity.

The software development industry embraced Agile, and it was not long before other industries started experimenting with Agile values and principles. Although Agile was intended for software developments, its values and principles could be applied to any team environment irrespective of the industry or the type of product or service they were developing. As a result, Agile methodology is increasingly used in many different industries with great success.

Scrum is an Agile framework that enables companies to adopt the Agile way of thinking without investing in prior experience and knowledge in Agile practices. While Agile does not provide steps to implement it, the Scrum framework provides clear steps on how to adopt Scrum practices making it easier for teams to adopt Agile.

The Scrum framework defines team roles, ceremonies, and artifacts that make it easier to adopt. Specific roles are given various responsibilities while Scrum ceremonies ensure that Agile principles of face-to-face interactions—providing customers with incremental versions of the product—and continuously improving as a team are achieved. Scrum artifacts provide the necessary documentation teams need; however, Agile methodology does not focus too much on documentation compared to traditional project management approaches.

The Kanban Method has its rules going all the way back to the Toyota factories in Japan, where it helped Toyota achieve high levels of productivity while reducing costs related to maintaining additional inventory. The Kanban method focuses on limiting *work in progress* where teams are encouraged to finish what they are working on before committing to new work. Teams are also encouraged to improve gradually, making Kanban very similar to the Agile way of thinking.

Lean Thinking is another philosophy that has many similarities to the Agile methodology. It focuses on helping processes increase productivity and profitability by reducing and eliminating wastes. Lean Thinking describes five principles that can be used to reduce and eliminate eight wastes resulting in the best use of resources. Lean Management has proven successful across several sectors and has fast become popular among many modern businesses.

Agile is a groundbreaking methodology that enabled teams to approach product development in an entirely different manner. It was able to solve many problems that the software development world was facing at the time and proved useful in many other sectors later on. Frameworks and methods such as Scrum, Kanban, and Lean share many similarities to Agile values and principles, but they are not the same. Agile, Scrum, Kanban, and Lean practices can be applied to different team environments depending on the projects, types of teams, and expectations involved to achieve project goals successfully.

Chapter 1: An Introduction to Project Management

Project management comprises time-sensitive goals assigned to a specific team and includes initiation, planning, execution, control, and closure of the project. Teams the world over, and across different sectors, use project management to achieve project-related goals with time constraints and predefined success criteria. These time constraints and success criteria are usually defined before the commencement of a particular project.

Scope, quality, time, and budget are the primary or key constraints of project management. In other words, the success of a project is gauged largely by how well it aligns with its expected or planned scope, quality, time, and budget. These constraints include the client's requirements and expectations and those of the company or organization the project team belongs to.

Client requirements and expectations are usually gathered and documented before a project begins. A clear understanding of those expectations and requirements enables the project stakeholders to form the project team that will create the end product to meet the predefined client requirements and expectations. Therefore, proper gathering and analysis of client requirements and expectations play a key role in determining a project's success.

A project is a temporary mission that is enforced to achieve a set of objectives during a specified period. Therefore, a project must have clear objectives regarding the product or service it will achieve. Furthermore, a project must also have a start and end date.

A project can create or make improvements to an existing product or service. A project can also be a one-time endeavor or an ongoing one. However, since a project needs to have a start and end date, an ongoing project is technically a project that repeats itself upon completion of its objectives.

For example, there may be a project where the objective is to manufacture a sports car according to strict guidelines in a month. The project team may complete the car in 29 days, bringing it to a closure. The same team might move on to the next project, which is the same: manufacturing the same car with the same requirements and time frame. Such projects are called ongoing projects.

Project management aims to utilize the resources available to a team to achieve project objectives without delays and to exceed the budget. The planning of resources includes personnel, finances, technology, and intellectual property. Project management also aims to meet predefined customer requirements and expectations while also facilitating some changes to those requirements and expectations along the way.

A project manager's job is to use a suitable project management methodology to initiate, plan, execute, control, and close the project within the allowed time frame. In most methodologies, the project manager determines when certain project components will be completed and which team members will contribute to those tasks. Some project management methodologies involve smaller teams making those decisions and initiating and executing tasks.

1.1 History of Project Management

Ancient records prove that officials were allocated management roles to complete different sections of the Great Pyramid of Giza built by the Pharaohs. The construction of the four faces of the Great Pyramid was assigned to different managers, who ensured they were completed on time. This would have involved planning, execution, and control.

The Great Wall of China is another enormous project that would have required a lot of management skills. Historical data indicate that the laborers were divided into three main groups or categories: soldiers, commoners, and criminals. These groups—that amounted to millions of people—were separately managed. Therefore, there is concrete evidence suggesting that some project management levels have been around for thousands of years.

The civil engineering industry in the 1950s first applied project management practices; however, they were limited to complex projects. The practices were not applied for smaller projects at the time. Over the next decade, project management expanded into many other engineering fields.

Henry Laurence Gantt, an American mechanical engineer who created the Gantt Chart in 1917, was one of the pioneers of scientific management and project management practices. Gantt charts became popular as a tool to guide projects, and he introduced many other techniques and tools to help plan and control projects. Henri Fayol, a French engineer, also introduced the five project management functions, which laid a foundation for project management for years to come.

The era of modern project management dawned in the 1950s, with many core engineering fields contributing towards its evolution. Project management was recognized as an important practice and discipline in many engineering sectors around this time. Gantt charts were used to manage most projects along with various informal tools before the 1950s. However, two project scheduling models emerged around this time that changed how project management was carried out.

This Critical Path Method (CPM) was one of those mathematical methods. It was developed through a joint venture between the Remington Rand Corporation and the DuPont Corporation. CPM quickly gained popularity and was used to manage plant maintenance projects.

The Program Evaluation and Review Technique (PERT) was the other project scheduling model that emerged. It was a model created by the U.S. Navy Special Projects Office along with Booz Allen Hamilton and the Lockheed Corporation for the Polaris missile submarine program. CPM and PERT have many similarities; however, they have numerous distinctions that make them more or less suitable for certain projects or industries.

CPM was used to manage projects that have predefined time frames for different tasks. PERT, on the other hand, was widely used in projects with uncertain time frames. Many private entities across different industries quickly started using CPM and PERT to manage different projects depending on their characteristics.

Different techniques were introduced to estimate and manage the cost of projects with Hans Lang dominating the way. The American Association of Cost Engineers was formed in 1956 by individuals and companies that used different project management tools and methodologies. The organization is now known as the Association for the Advancement of Cost Engineering (AACE). Practices that involve planning, cost estimation, scheduling, cost control, and project control have, for decades, been guided by the AACE.

The United States Department of Defense developed the concept of the Work Breakdown Structure (WBS) for the Polaris ballistic missile project. It was published upon completion of the project and mandated for use in future projects of the same size and scope. The WBS is a hierarchical structure for tasks and deliverables that need to be completed to close a particular project. The method was later adopted by the private sector and remains to be a highly useful project management tool to this date.

The International Project Management Association (IPMA) was formed in Vienna in 1965. It acted as a forum for project managers to share information, with more than 50 project management associations from across the world joining its network. The IPMA intends to develop the profession of project management with its membership exceeding 120,000 in 2012.

The Project Management Institute (PMI), formed in 1969 in the United States, aimed to improve the science, practice, and profession of project management. PMI's first symposium was held in Atlanta, Georgia, the same year with 83 attendees. Since then, the institute has taken giant strides by being highly recognized around the world for publishing *A Guide to the Project Management Body of Knowledge (PMBOK),* which acts as an essential tool for project managers. It includes different project management practices suitable for "most projects, most of the time."

The Project Management Institute also began issuing certifications for project management experts that highly contributed to the worldwide recognition of project management as a profession and expertise. PMI's two project management certifications are Project Management Professional (PMP) and Certified Associate in Project Management (CAPM).

Simpact Systems Limited created PROMPT II in 1975 as a response to the outcry for a solution to address projects extending delivery dates and exceeding budgets, especially in the IT industry. PROMPTII sets guidelines to the way stages flow in a computer project. The Government's Central Computing and Telecommunications Agency (CCTA) in the United Kingdom adopted PROMPT II for all of its information systems projects in 1979.

Author, philosopher, and business leader, Dr. Eliyahu M. Goldratt, introduced the Theory of Constraints (TOC) in his novel *The Goal* in 1984. The management philosophy was aimed at helping companies continuously achieve their goals. The theory aims to identify constraints that limit projects from achieving their goals. The process uses Five Focusing steps to restructure an organization around the constraints that are identified. The algorithms and philosophy behind TOC laid the foundation for the development of Critical Chain Project Management.

Scrum was recognized as a project management style in a paper titled "The New New Product Development Game," written by professors Hirotaka Takeuchi and Ikujiro Nonaka in 1986. Scrum was initially intended for the management of projects in software development. However, it later became popular as a general project management approach that was used in many different sectors.

Earned Value Management (EVM) was recognized as a project management technique only in the late 1980s and early 1990s; however, the concept has been used in factories since the dawn of the twentieth century. EVM became a key part of program management and procurement with the elevation of EVM leadership to the Undersecretary of Defense for Acquisition in 1989. EVM detected performance issues in the Navy McDonnell Douglas A-12 Avenger II program, which resulted in the program's cancellation by the Secretary of Defense, Dick Cheney, in 1991.

The PRojects IN Controlled Environments (PRINCE) method, developed from PROMPT II, was made the standard for all UK government information systems projects in 1989. However, PRINCE soon became known as a rigid approach that was only applicable to limited projects, such as larger ones.

Such limitations were addressed later in 1996 with the introduction of PRINCE2. While PRINCE was developed mainly for information technology and information systems projects, PRINCE2 was more generic. As a result, it was adopted by companies in many different sectors. PRINCE2 was also more applicable to projects of varying scales that contributed to its popularity.

Critical Chain Project Management (CCPM) was invented by Eliyahu M. Goldratt in 1997. It was based on algorithms and methods in Theory of Constraints (TOC) published by Goldratt in 1984. CCPM aims at maintaining even resources while ensuring flexibility when it comes to starting times of different tasks so that a project runs on schedule. PMBOK was recognized as a standard by the American National Standards Institute (ANSI) in 1998. The Institute of Electrical and Electronics Engineers (IEEE) also followed suit the same year.

Seventeen software experts gathered at The Lodge resort in Snowbird, Utah, in February 2001 to discuss and share knowledge regarding lightweight software development methodologies. This meet up resulted in the publication of the *Manifesto for Agile Software Development*. It defined the Agile approach, with some of the manifesto's authors going on to form the Agile Alliance, a non-profit organization focused on promoting software development in line with the twelve core principles introduced in the manifesto.

AACE International introduced the Total Cost Management Framework in 2006 that focused on applying the knowledge and skills of cost engineering. The fourth edition of the PMBOK Guide was released in 2008. A key revision of PRINCE2 took place in 2009, making the method more customizable and simpler. The updated method offers project managers seven principles to complete projects within budget, on time, and with the right quality.

The International Organization for Standardization in 2012 published *ISO 21500:2012, Guidance on Project Management*, as a result of work carried out over five years with contributions from experts from over 50 countries. The standard can be used by any organization, including private, public, or community, and any type of project irrespective of size, duration, and complexity.

The fifth edition of the PMBOK Guide was published in 2012. The fifth edition introduced characteristics and rules that are considered as good practice in project management. It also includes

Project Stakeholder Management, the tenth knowledge area in the guide, and four new processes for planning.

Chapter 2: Agile Project Management

Agile is a project management approach that is flexible and modern. It allows the breaking down of larger projects into simpler and manageable tasks that are then completed in short iterations known as *sprints*. Agile allows a team to adapt to change and complete work quickly.

The Agile project management approach may sound difficult to manage and somewhat complex. However, most companies, teams, and project managers often practice many approaches and principles of Agile without knowing so. Therefore, adopting Agile may not be as difficult as it may seem.

Agile was developed to solve different challenges that software development projects were facing at the time of its inception. However, today, Agile is used to manage projects, not only in the field of information technology but construction, education, marketing, and more. Therefore, many companies can benefit from adopting Agile irrespective of the sector they belong to.

Setting up and utilizing teams that follow the Agile methodology is usually simple, making it easier for organizations to adopt Agile. However, it is important to remember that every Agile team is different from another. Therefore, a thorough understanding of Agile basics is important so that Agile principles and values that work for that particular team can be emphasized and improved while ironing out the weak areas.

More traditional project management methodologies, such as the Waterfall model, approach a project where the end product is developed as a single piece. Agile, on the other hand, takes a different approach by breaking down the development of the product into smaller increments. Therefore, Agile requires less initial planning and design while being easier to manage and deliver on time while staying within the budget.

For example, the Waterfall project management method will approach the building of a house from start to end with one deliverable and delivery date in mind. However, when it comes to Agile, the house's construction is broken down into smaller pieces, such as the foundation, walls, roof, interior, and exterior. Each of these increments will have predefined due dates.

Breaking a larger project into smaller, more manageable chunks is something that many individuals practice every day. For example, someone would rarely clean their entire home as a single project with an idea of a time or date to end the work in mind. Instead, many break it into smaller *increments*: kitchen, living room, bedrooms, and so on. This helps them manage the work better and get things done quickly without trying to clean the entire house in one go.

Increments that products are broken down into are called *iterations* or *sprints* in Agile. These iterations are *time-boxed*, which means that they have a fixed start and end date, where the team works on achieving the predefined targets for that particular increment. An increment can last from one week to four weeks, depending on the practices followed by the team or organization.

Every iteration is handled by a *cross-functional* team. A cross-functional team is one that attends to planning, design, analysis, development, and testing. Therefore, team members possessing skills that are required for covering all these areas need to be included in an Agile team. For example, in a software development company, an Agile team should include business analysts, architects, developers, and quality assurance engineers.

The end of every iteration leaves a working product that can be brought to the stakeholders. This is one of the most important characteristics of Agile. A working version of the end product is maintained at the end of each iteration. Indeed, it may not have all the features of the end product; however, the stakeholders will be able to see the product being developed without having to wait until the end.

There are fewer risks associated with Agile project management because increments or working versions of the product are completed at the end of every iteration. Doing so enables the team to ensure that they are developing a product that meets client requirements and expectations.

Any mistakes or variations from requirements and expectations can be identified at the end of an iteration since the stakeholders can see a working version of the product. Fixing such issues is much less costly than identifying them at a later stage of product development or the very end.

For example, when a house is constructed using the Agile approach, the stakeholders will be able to see the foundation, walls, roof, etc., at the end of each increment. If there is anything that does not meet client requirements and expectations, it can be pointed out, and the team can fix those errors in the next iteration.

However, if the home is built using the Waterfall method, the client can only see a working version of the home at the end of construction. As such, if a certain characteristic of the roof does not agree with client requirements or expectations, the team will exceed the budget and time constraints and may need to redo some of the work on the interior and exterior while fixing the roof.

Agile methodology is also focused on enhancing communication among team members. It is prescribed that teams are accommodated close to each other in an office to communicate efficiently. This reduces the need for time-consuming communication methods such as calls, chats, and emails.

Every Agile team has a team member who represents that client. Stakeholders give consent to this particular team member to make decisions on their part when it comes to the work that is carried out by the team daily. The same person must also be available to answer any questions and provide clarifications whenever needed during iterations.

The end of an iteration provides a working version of the product or a product increment. The project team and stakeholders meet to review the product increment to ensure that the product that is being developed aligns with customer requirements and expectations. Agile is a project management methodology that can be used successfully in companies belonging to various sectors or industries. When properly implemented, it can bring teams toward highly satisfactory results.

2.1 What is The Manifesto?

Workers, companies, and clients became increasingly frustrated in the 1990s with existing project management methods such as the Waterfall. The end products were much different from the initial client requirements. Many projects were delayed while some were even canceled as clients were dissatisfied some of the companies' performances.

Most development teams were more concerned about documentation than developing products that met customer requirements and expectations. More importantly, traditional project management methodologies were unable to accommodate the changing demands of their customers well enough. Workers, specifically software developers, were also not as versatile.

There was a growing consensus in the software development industry that most companies were wasting resources by focusing on the less important things. The methods that were being used were not working for all projects, and a new methodology needed to be invented. An innovative and modern approach needed to be brought forth, so teams could be more independent and open to change, with higher productivity and efficiency.

As previously mentioned, seventeen individuals gathered at The Lodge in Snowbird. They went there to relax, eat, drink, ski, and, more importantly, find common ground. The result was the emergence of the Agile Manifesto for Software Development.

The document contained four core values and twelve principles that are prescribed for Agile software development. It was an alternative for project management methodologies largely driven by documentation and heavyweight processes that were proving to be unsuccessful for many types of projects.

This group, The Agile Alliance, published the *Agile Manifesto* that included the four values and twelve principles that they recommended for Agile software development. It must be noted that many Agile values and principles have been practiced by the experts belonging to the group for years. However, the manifesto made their vision more concrete that resulted in it taking the software development world by storm.

The team that worked on the *Agile Manifesto* included many experts and practitioners such as:

- Kent Back and Ron Jeffries, who co-created eXtreme Programming (XP)
- Andrew Hunt and Dave Thomas, who co-authored *The Pragmatic Programmer*
- Ken Schwaber and Jeff Sutherland, who co-created the Scrum framework
- Mike Beedle, co-author of *Agile Software Development with Scrum*
- Alistair Cockburn, the creator of Crystal Agile Methodology

- Jon Kern, who was a prominent lightweight process evangelist at the time
- Robert C Martin, also known as "Uncle Bob," a leading American software engineer and instructor
- Arie van Bennekum, the owner of Integrated Agile
- Martin Fowler, a partner at Thoughtworks
- Jim Highsmith, the creator of Adaptive Software Development (ASD)
- Brian Marick, an author and software testing expert
- Steve Mellor, inventor of Object-Oriented System Analysis (OOSA)
- Ward Cunningham, develop of the first Wiki
- James Grenning, author of Test-Driven Development

These men came up with the *Agile Manifesto* that would later change the way many companies manage projects.

2.2 Is Agile Only for Software Development?

It is fair to say that the majority of people aware of Agile project management have a background in the software development industry. Anyone who goes through the *Agile Manifesto* would clearly understand that the Agile methodology was intended for the software development practices. A look at the members of The Agile Alliance would also make it clear that the values and principles emerged in the software development world.

Agile may indeed have been created by a collective of software experts with the software development industry in mind. However, that does not limit Agile to the software industry because its values and principles can easily be applied to projects across a wide range of project types and industries.

Agile project management focuses on delivering value throughout the duration of a project instead of its very end. It is also highly open to change and better than many project management methodologies when it comes to responding to change. Agile also promotes creativity and innovation while maintaining the controlled development of products.

These are challenges that are present in not only software development but also in many other industries. Therefore, Agile can be used in numerous sectors and industries in addition to its popular use in software development.

2.3 Core Values and Principles of Agile

The Four Core Values of Agile

One of the main reasons for The Agile Alliance's gathering in 2001, and the *Agile Manifesto*, was to address many challenges that the software development industry was facing. Therefore, the four core values mentioned in the *Agile Manifesto* focus on what a team must do and avoid in an Agile environment. These four recommendations lay the foundation of how Agile teams function and how team members interact with each other and stakeholders.

Individuals and Interactions Over Processes and Tools

Agile methodology puts more value on people than tools and processes. The basic logic behind this value is that people and interactions involving people are easier to understand than tools and processes. It is a recognition of the optimal driving force of a development process, which is the human interactions instead of processes and tools.

When processes and tools drive the development of a product, the team becomes weaker when it comes to responding to change. As a result, they often fail to meet client requirements and expectations. However, when development is driven by individuals and their interactions, they can adapt to change better and, in return, are more likely to meet client requirements and expectations.

For example, processes and tools often unnecessarily complicate communication among individuals. However, when tools are taken out of the equation, and individuals are encouraged to communicate in person, communication becomes more effective and efficient. Agile also encourages communication whenever the need arises instead of following a process where communication is scheduled and limited to specific content. This contributes to teams being more responsive to change in Agile environments.

Working Software Over Comprehensive Documentation

There was an immense amount of documentation involved in the software development process when Agile was introduced to the world in 2001. Large amounts of time were dedicated to creating various documents, such as technical requirements, specifications, prospectus, user interfaced design documents, test and documentation plans, and approval documents. A substantial amount of documentation that existed in software development contributed to long delays in product development, with projects also exceeding budgets.

The *Agile Manifesto* emphasizes the delivery of working software instead of comprehensive documentation. Documentation is not entirely eliminated in Agile; however, it is streamlined so that those who contribute to the development of the product can work without being bogged down by documentation work.

Therefore, it must be highlighted that Agile does require some documentation, but it puts the main focus on delivering working versions of the product instead of documentation. For example, user stories are a type of document that enables developers to build new functionalities. Therefore, user stories are required in Agile.

Customer Collaboration Over Contract Negotiation

Before the inception of Agile project management, the project manager and customer would meet and negotiate when the product would be delivered and the details of the delivery. The requirements of the product are also negotiated in detail before any work is started. There would also be certain points in the project where they would meet and renegotiate according to the progress.

In project management methodologies such as Waterfall, the customer was involved in the process at the beginning and end. They were never involved during the time the product was being developed. There was a need for customer collaboration during the development phase of the product, and it was addressed by the *Agile Manifesto*.

Agile recommended that project managers collaborate with clients instead of contract negotiation. The customer is involved throughout the development process, making it easier for project managers and developers to deliver an end product that meets customer requirements and expectations. Agile may dictate the intervals where customers can collaborate, but some projects may involve customers attending all meetings, especially when it comes to complex projects.

Responding to Change Over Following a Plan

The change was considered an expense in traditional project management, especially in software development. As a result, most traditional project management methodologies put much emphasis on the development of elaborate plans. A lot of time and resources were allocated to gather customer requirements and expectations and design features that would meet those needs.

The idea was to do as much planning as possible so that there would be less change. The approach may have looked good on paper but lacked practicality. Customer requirements and expectations were often misunderstood or wrongly captured, which required changes even after investing a significant amount of resources to avoid such occurrences. Some customer requirements and expectations would also change during the development process, which required changes.

Therefore, many project managers started to realize that change was inevitable in software development. That may have resulted in the *Agile Manifesto* being more focused on responding to change instead of strictly following a plan. Agile project management requires teams to respond to change instead of avoiding it. The approach helps teams quickly come up with solutions while developing a more useful and satisfactory product.

The 12 Principles of Agile

As mentioned, the *Agile Manifesto* described twelve principles for teams to follow in the implementation of Agile project management. These principles are focused on creating and nurturing a culture that is more welcoming to change, with the customer being more involved in the development process, especially compared to traditional project management approaches. The principles also focus on making product development more aligned with the needs of businesses.

1. Customer satisfaction by early and continuous delivery of valuable software.

Traditional project management methodologies only allow the customer to use and experience the product upon its completion. The product is usually checked and tested thoroughly before it is brought in front of the customer. This means that the customer is left in the dark regarding the product until it has been completed. The customer is not usually involved during the product development phase, making it difficult for the development team to introduce changes to the product even if they feel that they are necessary.

Keeping the customer involved throughout the development of the product, especially at an early stage, is one of the best ways to make them happy. Customers are given small increments of the product at the end of each sprint from an early stage in development. They can take a good look at the product and request changes if needed. The development team can make those changes to the product without those changes costing too many resources.

In traditional project management approaches, there is a large gap between documentation and the completion of the product, at which point the customer provides feedback. However, in Agile, this gap is made shorter, with the customer frequently providing feedback so that the end product is something that the customer actually wants instead of what the customer planned for at the start of the project.

2. Welcome changing requirements, even in late development.

There is a chance that a customer's requirements and expectations are wrongly interpreted by project managers. In traditional project management, such mistakes would only be identified at the end of the project, requiring a large amount of work to make the necessary changes. In Agile project management, most changes are likely to be requested by customers when they can be managed with minimal resources.

Agile reminds teams that change is inevitable. Therefore, teams are more welcoming towards changing requirements instead of dreading them. When a change is requested, the teams attend to the change in the next iteration itself without it causing more damage or requiring more time to fix later on.

A request for a change by a customer during the latter stages of development usually means that the development team will need to put in an extra effort and time to make that change. However, Agile recommends that teams welcome changes, even in late development, so that a great product is developed while satisfying the customer.

3. Deliver working software frequently (weeks rather than months).

This principle requires that the iterative process in the Agile approach consists of smaller time frames, ideally every few weeks instead of months. Such an iterative process not only improves the performance of teams but also involves the customer more frequently. A working increment of the product is delivered at the end of each stage, at which point the customer will review it. The shorter the time frame between iterations, the more efficient teams will be and with less space for drifting away from customer requirements.

This principle is often confused with the first principle, which states that teams should focus on releasing working products early. However, the third principle highlights the importance of smaller and more constant releases. When a release is small, there is less space for mistakes. For example, in the software scenario, a smaller release might not result in the discovery of many bugs, and the customer may not need any changes. Even the bugs and changes that are agreed upon can be quickly fixed in the next iteration while making progress with the product.

Regular releases provide the customer with regular opportunities to provide feedback regarding the product that is being developed. If a working product is released every week, the team ends up receiving feedback every week from the customer, which helps them stay on track. If a working product is only released every two months, there is a higher chance of bugs and variations from the customer's expectations due to the lack of feedback that was received.

4. Close, daily cooperation between business people and developers.

One of the biggest downfalls of traditional project management methodologies is that most stakeholders are unaware of the product that is being developed during the development stage of the project. Those who directly contribute to the project's development are usually kept away from business people, including customers. For example, in traditional software development methodologies, software developers hardly interact with business people. This results in teams casually going through the development stages without the customer seeing the product they are shaping.

However, Agile recommends that stakeholders are more involved, especially during the development stages, so that an end product with great value can be developed with frequent feedback. Barriers that stood between the developers and business people are recommended to be taken down, with interaction with each other every day—doing so results in improved transparency, understanding, and respect.

5. Projects are built around motivated individuals who should be trusted.

One of the main reasons for many traditional project management failures is the micromanagement of team members by project managers and others. Micromanaging team members often decreases morale and acts as a barrier against creativity and innovation. Projects that are built around team members who lack motivation often end with disappointments.

Agile addresses this issue by placing trust in team members instead of micromanaging them. There is a good reason why the particular team has been assembled. Therefore, they require trust. Placing trust in teams motivates them to work efficiently and effectively. The work is monitored, but team members are left alone as much as possible.

In such an environment, team members are confident. They often voice their opinions and share their knowledge with others that paves the way for creative and innovative solutions. A motivated individual is a better team player. Therefore, Agile environments lead to improved team performance.

6. A face-to-face conversation is the best form of communication (co-location).

Traditional project management methodologies focused a lot on the documentation of conversations, scheduling meetings, email streams, and collaborative tools. However, such methods often cost time, despite seeming to be making teams more efficient. The *Agile Manifesto* identified this obstacle, and the solution was to recognize face-to-face interactions as the best form of communication.

In a more traditional environment, a team member may be more focused on documenting a conversation or its outcome instead of understanding it. There may be time lost in between emails, memos, and interactions using collaborative tools. Valuable time to take action may be lost while team members wait for the next scheduled meeting. All this can be solved with simple face-to-face conversations.

Many organizations indeed have employees who work remotely. Under such scenarios, face-to-face conversations may not look like the most practical way for teams to communicate. However, tools such as Skype and Zoom enables teams to communicate face-to-face irrespective of where they are physically. Therefore, in the modern world, a team does not need to be in the same room to have a face-to-face conversation.

7. Working software is the primary measure of progress.

Before the inception of Agile, different factors were used to measure the progress of a project. However, most of these factors simply encouraged teams to complete *tasks* and move on to the next one. There was very little attention to the product that was being made or how usable it was. It led to end products that lacked quality and did not meet customer requirements and expectations. Therefore, analysis, models, and elaborate mock-ups have very little meaning when compared to a working product.

Agile prescribes that progress is measured based on the available working product instead of other factors, such as the number of tasks that have been completed. Thus, the progress of a project can be measured by how far the working product has evolved. Agile encourages teams to remain focused on what is more important: the working product. The working product is going to satisfy the customer.

8. Sustainable development, able to maintain a constant pace.

Working on complex and long projects often result in team members burning out after functioning at their best over a lengthy period. Many projects often start fast but lose pace as they move further into the development phase. Therefore, sustaining a constant development pace was one of the main areas that Agile wished to address.

The eighth principle in the *Agile Manifesto* dictates that the development speed needs to be sustainable throughout the course of the project. Therefore, teams are recommended not to undertake any more work than they can sustain over a long period. Working hard is encouraged, but overworking themselves is discouraged altogether.

The repeatable iterative pattern in Agile helps teams establish a healthy development pace where they are efficient without overtaxing themselves with too much work. An iteration should not have less or more work than any other; every iteration should involve just the right amount of work. Maintaining such a consistent and sustainable development speed keeps team members free of stress while the project progresses at an acceptable pace.

9. Continuous attention to technical excellence and good design.

It is natural for most businesses to consider lengthy production times as a cost. The longer a product takes to build, the longer a company needs to wait to be paid and start building the next product. Furthermore, many businesses believe that the end-user does not really care about their technical excellence. Technical excellence, in most cases, does not generate a direct income for a company. However, that does not mean companies should focus less on it.

If drawing a good technical design for a product is neglected, it might affect the product speed. Without a good design, a product will be difficult to make and hence take more time. Furthermore, products with poor designs are usually more difficult or even impossible to change concerning changing customer requirements and expectations.

When it comes to small projects, it might make sense to develop the product instead of spending a lot of time designing it. However, complex projects require teams to focus on technical quality and great design. Great design does not need to be created before the development of the product begins. The design can evolve as the product is developed. However, teams need to be provided with the time and resources to do so.

Agile nurtures good designs and technical excellence by encouraging teams to improve their work after every iteration. Anything that needs to be fixed must be fixed now without having to come back later. The team is also expected to learn from mistakes and improve so that the same mistakes are not repeated, costing valuable resources. Focusing on great designs and technical quality adds immense value to a product. Customers will take notice, and the business will soon start benefiting since satisfied customers often help companies.

10. Simplicity—the art of maximizing the amount of work not done—is essential.

It is safe to say that Agile is a project management methodology that is more focused on getting work done and adding more value to products instead of formalities. Many procedures followed traditionally in companies may no longer be relevant in an Agile environment. Teams might opt to ignore certain procedures, automate time-consuming manual tasks, and use existing libraries instead of writing their own.

Doing all this gives teams more time to focus on the work that needs to be done and add more value to the product they are developing. The aim is to move as quickly as possible by eliminating unnecessary complexities. Teams are encouraged to keep things as simple as possible. Simplicity has proven to be a great ingredient when it comes to streamlining processes. In any iteration, tasks that need to be completed are the main focus of every team member. Documenting, planning, and adding extra features are not considered as priorities until the work that needs to be done is completed.

11. Best architectures, requirements, and designs emerge from self-organizing teams.

This principle is aimed at making some of the earlier principles realistic in working environments. How Agile recommends that developers and businesses communicate directly and regularly and why working software is more important than theoretical models was discussed earlier. How motivated individuals contribute to producing high-quality products was also established above. By comparison, this states that, for all this to succeed, teams must be allowed to self-organize themselves without too much control from above.

In an Agile environment, teams are given the power to organize everything related to product development. They decide when they want to communicate, how the tasks are completed, how the work is going to be divided among team members, and more. Such an environment is considered to enhance productivity and quality since those who directly develop the product start to take more ownership.

There is a big difference between being held responsible and taking ownership of a product that is being developed. When an individual is being held responsible for a certain task, there is a sense of obligation and stress around it. However, taking ownership of the work that someone does comes from within themselves. It is a choice instead of something that's assigned by a superior. As a result, teams tend to be more efficient and effective when left to function independently.

12. Regularly, the team reflects on how to become more effective and adjusts accordingly.

Agile project management methodology recommends that teams take the time to regularly look at themselves and the work they have been doing so that they can make collective and individual improvements and adjustments to be more effective in the future. Expecting a self-organizing team to be perfect is unrealistic, no matter how well qualified the team members. Therefore, teams must be encouraged to reflect on themselves and identify areas that they can improve on.

In Agile environments, teams usually complete a product increment during an iteration and pause. Then, they will take a bit of time to reflect on the previous iteration. During these sessions, team members will identify areas that they can improve on, both as a team and as individuals. Then they will proceed to the next iteration.

Therefore, Agile methodology reduces complacency in teams. Being complacent is one of the biggest mistakes an individual, team, or company can make in any business, be it software development or manufacturing. Agile reduces complacency by requiring teams to continuously and regularly improve themselves by reflecting on their most recent work.

Project managers often promote sessions where teams evaluate their work and performance and discuss ways to improve. Doing so benefits companies since teams become more productive while also evolving, with individuals gaining more skills. Furthermore, products also increase in value as mistakes are avoided throughout the development as teams become more capable.

2.4 What Does an Agile Team Look Like?

A small group of individuals assigned to the same effort or project is considered a *team* in an Agile environment. Most individuals who belong to Agile teams are usually full-time employees. However, part-time specialists may join an Agile team and contribute to the project if the need arises.

The idea of a team brings shared accountability to that group of people. It does not matter if the outcomes of their efforts are good or bad; the entire team is attributed to them instead of narrowing things down to any member of the team. It is recommended that an Agile team possesses all the required skills and expertise that are required to develop a product.

For example, a team that is developing software must include programmers, architects, and testers, as well as individuals with business and domain knowledge, such as business analysts. Results are given more weight in Agile development instead of roles and responsibilities.

Therefore, a software programmer may complete certain tasks traditionally considered someone else's responsibility, such as requirement and performance analysis and testing. The focus is on getting the work done instead of limiting team members to specific roles and responsibilities.

One of the most common errors that many companies make when implementing Agile is mistaking a *team* as a *group*. A group of people working together may not always be an Agile team. Furthermore, a group member may contribute to multiple projects simultaneously without considering them to be in more than one *team*. A group of people may also be any number above three.

In an Agile environment, a team should have a minimum of three members and ideally, a maximum of ten members. Agile teams are usually co-located—or they function at their best when they are co-located. Members of an Agile team are dedicated to a single project on a full-time basis. They should not be spread across more than one project at the same time.

Agile teams are cross-functional, which means that they can function on their own without depending on individuals who do not belong to the team. That is why an Agile team should possess all the skills and expertise to complete the tasks that it is assigned. Agile teams usually have a limited number of team roles according to the Agile framework that is being used.

For example, Scrum is an Agile framework, and an Agile team using the Scrum framework needs to have individuals filling the roles of Scrum Master, Product Owner, and Team Members.

Collaboration with Customers

Agile teams regularly and continuously interact with the customer. The methodology states that the development team must provide a working version of the product as early as possible. This is usually available at the end of the first iteration, where the customer can review the product increment and provide feedback. Any changes that are needed are also identified and requested, reducing the need for costly changes.

The customer interacts with an Agile team throughout the development phase. They communicate swiftly, and the customer's requirements and expectations are easily understood by the team compared to solely referring to documents. Face-to-face interaction with the team also helps customers explain their requirements clearly without being misunderstood. Even if they are misunderstood, the mistakes can be corrected at the end of the next iteration.

Compared to traditional project management methodologies, such as Waterfall, Agile is preferred by customers as they communicate directly with the development team instead of someone who represents them. Information is unlikely to be misinterpreted as a result. Regular and continuous interactions between Agile teams and customers also pave the way for developing high-quality products with great value.

Daily Communication

There is a big difference between a group of people who work together and a *team*. A team is a cohesive unit that efficiently communicates and collaborates to achieve a set of goals. The quality of teamwork is determined by six key components: coordination, communication, balanced contributions, support, cohesion, and effort. Teamwork quality directly impacts a team's performance and the success of the project.

Agile methodology believes that teams are more successful when members of those teams rely on each other instead of various tools and processes. Working together as a team gives team members the power and boldness to come up with innovative solutions instead of following traditional methods. Therefore, teamwork is one of the most important ingredients of Agile methodology.

Agile teams plan and organize their work among themselves by quick daily meetings. They are also encouraged to have face-to-face conversations whenever needed instead of waiting for the next scheduled meeting or relying on other mediums, such as chats, emails, and collaborative tools. Team members are located in the same area close to each other to facilitate face-to-face conversations. The team often invites stakeholders for brainstorming meetings who might help them with valuable inputs.

The entire Agile team connects at daily meetings to become aware of their progress and any issues. These face-to-face encounters are quick and to the point. At times, problems that certain team members are facing may be brought up with the entire team collaboratively making plans to overcome those obstacles. Such collaboration and trust build teamwork while positively contributing to the progress of the project. The focus of daily communication also makes Agile more sustainable.

Motivated Individuals

Motivation is one of the most important ingredients in maintaining productivity and performance throughout the development phase of a project. It becomes more important as the size, complexity, and the duration of the project increases. Motivation drives teams toward putting in their best effort every day for an extended length of time without burning out.

Agile environments aim to give individuals plenty of motivation to work toward the goals of their teams collaboratively. They are passionate about the work they do. They also do their work while supporting their team members, as achieving the goals of an individual is not considered a success in an Agile setting. Fueled by motivation, support, trust, and consistency, Agile teams often establish highly productive rhythms sustained throughout projects resulting in highly satisfactory outcomes.

Creating an environment to nurture motivated team members is not easy, especially if a team is new to Agile. Most companies start with changing their floor plans to open offices. Teams can perform efficiently in such settings as their team members are just a few steps away whenever they need to have a quick conversation. Such a floor plan also encourages team members to collaborate more and enhance brainstorming among teams while keeping individuals focused on team activities.

It is important to realize that Agile teams achieve progress through individual work. Therefore, individual workspaces also need to be available for team members. They provide a quieter area, which can be used to perform individual work toward the team goal.

Self-Organizing Teams

Teams are trusted to organize how they will complete the work they wish to achieve during an iteration in Agile. They decide how the work is going to be executed and who is going to do which tasks. There is no involvement from the management regarding assigning tasks to team members or tracking tasks assigned to individuals. An

Agile team is completely trusted by the management to make the right decisions.

It is an arrangement that everyone involved needs to appreciate. Managers can stop pushing people to do their work. Workers can stop managers from looking over their shoulders all the time. The arrangement needs team members to be very confident about their work. They must also be prepared to overcome obstacles that might arise. However, they can take comfort in knowing that their team members will be there to support them.

Accountability and responsibility are shared equally among all team members of an Agile team. As a result, they are required to perform both as individuals and in team roles. Each member needs to complete the work that is assigned to them by the team. Furthermore, they must be willing to step outside of their individual roles to overcome obstacles as a team whenever one or more team members are faced with difficulty.

When a team fails to meet the expected goals during an iteration, they identify the mistakes and learn. There is no direction from the management. Improvement is organically created within the team and, commonly, newly formed Agile teams have an Agile mentor.

It takes teams some time to become self-organizing without running into problems. Coaching and training need to be provided so that teams learn about how Agile works and improves as the project moves on. Even a team that is functioning very well may benefit from the existence of an Agile mentor as it enables team members to improve.

Agile teams are also given the freedom to determine what tools and processes they are going to follow. The tools and processes they choose may differ from those used by other teams in the same company. The company can provide the tools; however, the team is not entitled to request training on how to use the tools and processes that they choose to work with.

Continuous Improvements as Teams

Agile teams need to regularly and routinely reflect on their performance so they can improve. As a result, Agile teams are dedicated to continuous improvement. Naturally, Agile teams do not respond well to commands and orders. However, they are more open to coaching and mentoring. Retrospectives are sessions that are scheduled routinely after the completion of an iteration to facilitate team improvement.

During such sessions, team members talk about the things that went both well and wrong. They then collectively identify ways to improve the process while avoiding mistakes, so the next iteration runs smoothly. Great Agile teams use retrospectives to their advantage, as continuous improvements not only make their lives easier but also improve their skills and benefit their organization.

It may take Agile teams some time to gauge their optimal performance levels while keeping sustainability in mind. Newly formed teams are prescribed to go slow in the beginning and gradually increase the amount of work they take on during every iteration. Furthermore, these increments to the workload need to stop when they feel their maximum capacity is met. Continuous improvement does not mean that teams need to take on a larger workload.

Instead, teams are encouraged to understand the most work they can do while sustaining productivity. Many teams that undertake larger workloads experience burnouts, where team members are overworked and too stressed. Therefore, the workload that an Agile team undertakes needs to be such that the same level of productivity can be maintained for a long time—at least until the project is completed. Furthermore, teams need to keep a buffer for unplanned work and unexpected events that might come their way.

2.5 Agile Team Roles

Agile is a project management methodology introduced to solve many problems companies and clients face using traditional project management methods. The approach is focused on breaking goals down into smaller, independent products that can be incrementally developed and released. The Agile workflow requires highly coordinated teams to keep up with demanding schedules and short task spans. As a result, Agile team roles need to be well defined and understood by every team member.

Team Lead (Team Coach or Project Lead)

This individual is responsible for providing an Agile team with coaching and guidance. The team leader also needs to obtain the resources the team needs and remove any factors that harm the team and its performance. The role of the team leader does not involve much planning as the entire team works on planning.

Many wrongly think that a team lead is the manager of an Agile team; however, the role does not reflect a rank. It instead reflects responsibility and knowledge that are used to guide an Agile team in the right direction.

The Product Owner

An individual who has a good sense and vision about the end product being developed is usually trusted with the Product Owner role. He or she is often a key stakeholder or an executive in a company. The Product Owner must guide a team through the development process while correcting mistakes and initiating changes whenever required.

In an Agile environment, the Product Owner is considered to have a role similar to the captain of a ship. The captain directs the ship on the correct path while establishing order among the ship's crew. The captain also has the final word on any changes that need to be made aboard the ship.

The Product Owner provides a team with similar guidance and direction by carrying out a range of duties. One of the most important responsibilities of a Product Owner is to define the work that must be done. The Product Owner makes project objectives clear and transparent to a team while setting standards in terms of the work quality that needs to be delivered.

The work that the team completes shapes the end product. However, the Product Owner is responsible for creating tasks that will take the team there. A Product Owner is usually an individual who is passionate about the product and has a clear idea and vision about why the product needs to exist. Such an individual will instantly know when the product is not being shaped right.

Product Owners need to be very good at communicating with the team as a collective and with individual team members. They must maintain clarity and transparency at high levels so that the entire team is on the same page regarding the product they are developing. Therefore, the Product Owner participates in daily stand-up meetings of an Agile team and can also call any one-on-one ad hoc meetings if they feel it necessary.

The Product Owner is responsible for ensuring that the work done by the team is flowing smoothly. Furthermore, the Product Owner must ensure that the end product is in its most valuable form. They must also understand the priority of tasks that need to be completed based on project circumstances as well as feedback from stakeholders.

The Product Owner also must ensure that the team can deliver project iterations continuously with precise cycle planning. The end goal of a Product Owner is to make sure that the development process brings value for customers and other stakeholders to develop a product of value. The Product Owner is required to maintain communications with the development team, end-users, partners, and business executives throughout the project.

The Team Member

Workers with diverse expertise are known as team members. They directly contribute to the development of a product. Front-end and back-end software developers, designers, copywriters, architects, and videographers can all be members of a team in a particular sector where their expertise is used to develop a product. Team members may have different skills, but they are all responsible for getting the work done.

The majority of an Agile team is made up of team members. If the Product Owner is the ship's captain, the team members are the crew. It is natural for team members to bring a variety of skills, expertise, and traits to an Agile team. Individuals who are creative and can work autonomously usually thrive in Agile environments.

A team member is considered a *specialist* who contributes to the development of the product. Team members must work both collaboratively and independently. They can consult each other for brainstorming or meet with the Product Owner to find answers to any questions they might have. They must also work efficiently while avoiding distractions.

In Agile, team members are given a lot of freedom to direct and organize themselves and their work. Therefore, it is safe to say that most individuals feel empowered in an Agile environment, leading them to take ownership of their work. This usually results in individuals performing much better compared to traditional project management styles. Agile also encourages teams to improve continuously, and some of the positive effects also contribute to the personal development of team members.

Stakeholders

It is true that the stakeholder does not directly contribute to the development of the product, and are not always involved. However, stakeholders play an important role when it comes to shaping the end product that is being developed by an Agile team. A stakeholder can be a business executive, end-user, investor, production support staff member, external auditor, or a team member from another team.

Stakeholders are usually picked depending on the inputs they can provide or are required for the smooth functioning of an Agile team. The inputs also often affect the project direction. Successful stakeholders can help Agile teams develop products that meet business goals and end-users' expectations. Furthermore, stakeholders can, at times, address certain challenges that are experienced by team members.

Representatives from legal departments, customers, technical experts, account managers, marketing experts, salespeople, and many other professionals can be considered stakeholders of a project depending on its nature and the nature of the product. Stakeholders provide valuable insights regarding the end product and the way it is meant to be used. It is common for stakeholders to work collaboratively with Product Owners during an iteration and provide feedback when the released product increment is reviewed.

Agile Mentor

Individuals who act as coaches and mentors for teams that are new to Agile are known as Agile Mentors. Therefore, an Agile Mentor must have a vast amount of experience with Agile projects. They must also share their knowledge with an Agile team by providing coaching and mentoring instead of giving out orders and commands.

Mentors are instrumental in helping new project teams understand how Agile works and achieve high-performance levels. The Agile Mentor is merely there to provide guidance and direction to an Agile team. He or she will not contribute to the development process. Thus, the role of an Agile Mentor is an optional one.

Additional Agile Roles for Larger Projects

The roles that were described above are common in Agile teams. However, some companies may include more Agile roles, especially when working on larger and more complex projects. A good example is the inclusion of domain and technical experts to ensure that the development team does not experience any gaps in knowledge and expertise in terms of domain and technology.

It is also common for testing and audit teams to join Agile teams. These teams work with the Agile team throughout the development process to provide them assistance with testing and auditing.

Independent testing teams are useful when testing complex products where there is a high chance of coming across mistakes that testers in the Agile team may miss. Therefore, the presence of such individuals aids in the product development process.

When it comes to a project that involves multiple sub-systems that are handled by separate independent Agile teams, an Integrator is brought in so that sub-systems are integrated properly and to a sound plan. The Integrator ensures that sub-systems are tested properly and might even bring in external testing teams if the need arises.

Some complex projects may require an experienced architect. An Architect Owner is included in Agile teams for such projects where the Architect Owner makes plans and takes care of decision-making. The roles of Architect Owner and Integrator may exist in the same project if it involves complex, multiple sub-systems.

2.6 What Is the Overall Goal of Agile?

Agile is a modern approach to project management that intends to: make project management simpler, avoid long delays, and ensure that products are not different from customer requirements and expectations. It is a flexible approach that allows projects to be broken down into smaller and easily manageable tasks. These tasks are included in short iterations that have specific start and end dates. The development team focuses on completing the tasks within the iteration.

At the end of every iteration, a working or usable version of the product is brought forward to the customer. This enables the customer to see and use working versions of the product regularly, especially starting from a very early stage in development. As a result, the client is in regular agreement about the product that is being built. Any changes that are required are added to the next iteration.

The Agile method allows teams to organize themselves and deliver work fast. They can also quickly respond to change. Teams can quickly re-evaluate the current circumstances and adjust the work they are going to do in an increment instead of trying to keep to a plan during the entire product development phase. Agile methodology teaches teams to embrace change instead of avoiding it. As a result, Agile methodology has been highly successful in projects with changing requirements.

Agile may look like a complex methodology to anyone new to it. It might also seem difficult to manage. On the contrary, Agile is one of the most straightforward methodologies out there that make managing teams much easier.

Another goal of Agile is to create an environment where creativity is encouraged. Some projects may begin without the end product clearly defined. Such projects need teams that can quickly adapt to change and come up with creative solutions and ideas. The Agile approach is highly suited for such projects that involve high levels of change, creativity, and innovation.

The Agile approach was originally intended for software development. However, it has been successfully adopted by companies in different sectors since the Agile values and principles can be applied to any industry. As a result, it is common to see the Agile methodology in motion in education, marketing, military, construction, and automotive industries.

Agile intends to create shorter development cycles instead of being limited to a single or too few cycles during the product development phase. As a result, Agile provides frequent releases. These shorter cycles help teams to respond to any changes requested by the client easily. Agile project management involves a basic process that includes a range of activities, such as project planning, the creation of the product roadmap, planning of releases and iterations, daily stand-up meetings, reviews, and retrospectives.

Project Planning

A project needs to begin with a clear plan. Although Agile involves less planning than traditional project management approaches, it still requires a certain level of planning. Project planning in Agile includes understanding the project's end goal, the project's value to the client, and how the end goal is going to be achieved.

Some individuals also develop a project scope; however, it is important to remember that project scope is subject to change since the purpose of Agile is to embrace change. Therefore, the likelihood of features being added or removed from a project scope is high in Agile.

Product Roadmap Creation

This activity breaks the end product into a set of features. These features must create the end product once combined since the team will develop each of those features during iterations. Therefore, if the end product is not broken down into the correct features, the team may face difficulties towards the end of the project while posing the risk of delays.

The Product Backlog is also developed at this point. The Product Backlog lists all the features that should be in the final product according to customer requirements and expectations. Teams use the Product Backlog to choose tasks that they are going to complete in a particular iteration. Therefore, the Product Backlog must be complete so that any tasks or features are not missed.

Release Planning

Traditional project management methodologies such as the Waterfall method only involve one release, provided on the implementation date. Agile, on the other hand, involves many short development cycles. As a result, features of the end product are released at the end of every cycle. Creating a plan for these releases is advised. Release plans may change while the project runs its course. Therefore, it is recommended that the release plan is revisited before the start of every iteration or development cycle.

Iteration Planning

Agile teams usually plan what will be done during an iteration by choosing tasks from the Product Backlog. The team then decides which team member will contribute to each task while ensuring that tasks are distributed evenly between the entire team. Teams are encouraged to visually track the workflow, using whiteboards and similar methods, to maintain transparency and understanding among the team. The visual representation of tasks also helps teams identify and eliminate bottlenecks.

Daily Meetings

The Agile methodology prescribes daily meetings where the team gets together and assesses the work that has been completed and the work that remains in the current iteration. They then collectively make plans for the day while ensuring that they are on track to complete all the tasks in the iteration on time.

It is recommended that daily meetings are only limited to fifteen minutes. Furthermore, they should not serve the purpose of brainstorming or problem-solving. Their purpose is to simply review the tasks at hand and determine what the team will achieve within the day. Agile environments encourage daily stand-up meetings since sitting down usually causes meetings to drag.

Reviews and Retrospectives

Agile is a project management methodology that is intended to reduce the chances of the end product varying from the original customer requirements and expectations. This is achieved with the customer being provided working increments of the product throughout the development phase. Every cycle or iteration that is completed provides the customer with a working version of the product that they can review.

Therefore, the customer is aware of the product that is being developed from an early stage of the development process and can identify any changes that need to be made. Such changes are easier and less costly to make compared to identifying changes at the end of development. Therefore, reviews are a key part of Agile development.

The Agile methodology also encourages teams to seek ways to continue regularly. As a result, retrospectives are held at the end of each iteration. During a retrospective, team members reflect on what went right and wrong during the iteration. They then discuss how they are going to improve as a team during the next iteration.

2.7 How Is Agile Different Than Other Methodologies

The Agile project management methodology was introduced to solve many of the challenges experienced in software development with traditional project management methods. As a result, Agile introduced a novel approach compared to many of those traditional project management methodologies, with several differences between them.

Concurrent Development and Testing

Agile breaks down the end product into smaller increments. The team then works on developing each of these product increments during iterations that last for a fixed amount of time. During an iteration, development and testing happen at the same time. Concurrent development and testing allow better communication among developers, testers, managers, and customers.

This was a major difference that Agile introduced compared to traditional methods, such as the Waterfall Model or Linear Sequential Life Cycle Model. The Waterfall Model follows a sequential order where the development team moves on to a stage upon the completion of the other. As a result, testing begins upon the completion of the previous step, which usually is development. Therefore, development and testing do not happen concurrently in the Waterfall method.

Stages are Repeated in Cycles

Agile breaks down the product development phase into cycles or iterations. Key parts of product development, including planning, development, and testing, are involved in every cycle. Once a cycle is completed, the team moves on to the next cycle, where key steps, including planning, development, and testing, occur again.

Methods such as Waterfall, on the other hand, are strictly sequential. It involves eight stages where the completion of one stage enables the team to move on to the next. However, once the team moves on to a certain stage upon the completion of another, they cannot go back. Therefore, if a change is discovered towards the end of the process, their model does not define a way to facilitate it.

The Waterfall method originated and became highly popular in the construction and manufacturing sectors. Processes in these industries are structured where changes are usually rare and unfeasible. Therefore, changes are not accommodated in such industries. The Waterfall method is suitable for such processes where there is a low chance of change. Such processes also allow for detailed documentation that the Waterfall method requires.

Prior Experience and Knowledge

The use of traditional project management methods does not require team members to have prior knowledge. Methods such as Waterfall are very easy to follow even for an individual who has not been part of a Waterfall project before. In most cases, the Waterfall method can be used with the presence of an experienced project manager.

Agile, on the other hand, requires prior knowledge. Team members, customers, and company leaders need to know how Agile works and things they should and should not do in an Agile environment. The difference between the way things are done in a traditional environment and an Agile environment also contributes to this need for Agile knowledge.

Individuals who play roles, such as team leads, product owners, team members, and stakeholders, all need to understand their roles clearly. They must also be aware of Agile values and principles for the methodology to be successful. As a result, most companies that are new to Agile introduce Agile Mentors to their teams so the team members can be guided and directed in the right direction.

Enforcing Discipline vs. Trust and Freedom

Project management methodologies such as the Waterfall method are strict about how things and done and when they are done. Discipline is enforced with strict guidelines on focusing on requirements, comprehensive documentation, and following the sequence of phases strictly irrespective of the project and customer needs. Although the method is a well-documented approach that enables stakeholders and customers to understand the product, it may not be practical in many instances.

For example, if a team misses an important feature of the project during development, which is only discovered at the testing phase, there is no way for the team to go back and develop that feature. However, it may play a key role in the product. Enforcing discipline fails in such instances.

Agile, on the other hand, gives teams the freedom to get things done so that a great product is created. In what sequence activities take place does not concern Agile. Agile teams are trusted by the management to function independently and make the right decisions to complete a product full of value.

Avoiding Change vs. Embracing Change

The way that traditional project management methods approach change is their drawback and the reason behind the invention of the Agile methodology. Most traditional methods try to avoid change through extensive analysis, planning, and documentation. This is because most such methodologies are linear or sequential. The teams cannot switch between phases. Therefore, there is no space to accommodate changes in such methods.

Agile, on the other hand, takes an approach where change is embraced. The approach consists of smaller and regular development cycles that produce usable iterations of the product that the project is gradually building. The testers can test and find bugs and mistakes before the end of the iteration, while the customer also gets the chance to see the product increment and provide feedback. Such interactions sometimes result in changes being made to the product. However, Agile teams have a mindset where such changes are welcomed since they increase the end product's value.

The Delivery of Working Software

Most traditional project management methodologies do not deliver a working product until the end of the project. As a result, customers only get the chance to see the product once it has been completed. Such an approach may only work where the customer exactly knows the product they need. However, this is not the case most of the time, and that was one reason that inspired the introduction of the *Agile Manifesto.*

Most traditional project management methodologies are focused on gathering customer requirements and analyzing them at the beginning of the project. Then these requirements are comprehensively documented. The development of the product does not begin until all these stages are complete. Then the customer needs to wait a long time until the end of the project to see a working product.

However, most traditional methods do not account for the fact that the customer requirements and expectations can change during the project. Therefore, they may not see much value in the product they needed at the start of the project. Therefore, traditional project management methods do not accommodate or suit projects where there is a high chance of changing requirements.

Agile, on the other hand, is focused on developing working increments of the product regularly. More importantly, the development begins early with the client being able to see releases from an early stage of the project without waiting until the end. As a result, any changes that the customer wishes to be made can be easily completed in the next iteration. The delivery of working versions at regular intervals makes Agile a great methodology to develop products with ever-changing requirements or if a customer is not certain about the product they need.

Team Characteristics

There are significant differences between teams in traditional project management methodologies and Agile. Important attributes are the definition of a team, the way teams operate, team leadership, the types of experts that belong to a team, and many others.

Agile teams have very little structure, while most other teams are structured with permanent team members and roles. Agile team members are interchangeable. As a result, the work is completed faster. The self-organizing quality of Agile teams eliminates the need for project managers in Agile environments. However, most other project management methodologies require the guidance and management expertise of project managers.

Agile teams do not feature team members with different ranks. Every member of the team is treated with the same level of respect, and the work is evenly distributed among all team members. Other management methods feature teams where ranks are involved, and micromanagement of teams is present.

An Agile team consists of all kinds of experts that are needed to develop a product without relying on anyone outside of the team. However, other project methodologies may instead focus on creating teams based on expertise. Such teams are provided targets to achieve by their superiors. However, Agile teams organize themselves; they select the workload that they are going to achieve in an iteration.

Most traditional project management approaches do not involve or require high levels of team coordination. However, Agile requires teams to coordinate to the best of their abilities so that goals can be met collaboratively. Team members are encouraged to support each other as they pull their weight in an Agile environment.

Funding and Risk

Traditional project management methodologies are usually considered safe to manage fixed-price projects. Risk agreements are signed at the beginning of such projects that result in reduced risks. However, when Agile is used for fixed-price projects, it may become stressful for the company, especially if continuous changes delay the project or if the project's completion takes longer than the company estimated. The Agile methodology works best with projects that have non-fixed funding. The client agrees to pay the company for its resources, even if estimated delivery dates need to be extended since the focus is on developing a product full of value.

Requirements and Changes

When it comes to more traditional project management methods, requirements are gathered, analyzed, and agreed upon at the beginning of the project. This phase is usually completed and thoroughly documented before the development of the product. The developers then refer to documented requirements and develop the product. Upon the completion of the development, the testing begins. The developers then fix any bugs detected by the testers, and the product is delivered to the client.

If there is a misunderstanding during the initial requirements gathering stage about a requirement, the client only gets to find out at the end of the project. This may happen due to confusion. The client may also change his or her mind about a certain requirement while the product is in development. Some changes in the business environment might also make certain features of the product less effective. However, traditional project management approaches do not consider such scenarios due to their linear approach to product development.

Agile, on the other hand, requires the Product Owner to regularly prepare requirements upon receiving feedback from the customer at the end of every iteration. Neither the development team nor the customer completely relies on the requirements gathered before starting the project. Requirements and changes are established as the product is developed incrementally.

There are numerous advantages that this approach offers both the development team and the customer. The product that is being developed offers more value to the customer. As a result, the customer is likely to be more satisfied with the project. Any lapses in requirement analysis can be quickly accounted for without costing the company much, since the customer is more involved in the development process, increasing the chances of correcting such mistakes.

Chapter 3: Scrum Project Management

The Agile methodology emerged as a result of the failures of prominent and popular project management methodologies. The linear and sequential nature of those methodologies and the focus on documentation were seen as disadvantages, especially when it came to complex projects with high probabilities of change.

The Agile Alliance introduced the *Agile Manifesto* that declared four values and twelve principles that aimed to change the way projects were managed in the software development industry.

Most of the values and principles were different from what was mentioned in the Project Management Body of Knowledge (PMBOK). There was a greater emphasis on communication, teamwork, collaboration, team independence, the delivery of functioning software in increments, and the ability to adapt to change. The Agile approach was also one of the earliest methodologies to embrace change as it was a reality in business; however, most traditional methods considered change to be costly.

Scrum is an Agile framework that enables teams to efficiently and effectively work on projects in unison. The framework takes many Agile values and principles a step further, enabling teams to function at their best. Scrum framework describes specific meetings, tools, and roles that can be used to help teams organize and manage their work efficiently and productively.

Important team traits, such as learning from experience, working on a problem independently, and reflecting on wins and losses in search of improvement, are highlighted in Scrum. While the Scrum framework initially gained immense popularity in software development, it soon proved to apply to all kinds of teams across sectors and industries with great success. As a result, the framework became very popular.

Although Scrum is merely an Agile framework, it is often mistaken as a project management methodology. Furthermore, many individuals wrongly think that Scrum and Agile are the same approaches. Certain Agile values and principles have indeed been inspired by Scrum. For example, Scrum's focus on continuous improvement through regular team reflecting on wins and losses is one of the principles described in the *Agile Manifesto.*

However, Scrum and Agile are not the same approach or methodology. While Agile methodology is more of a mindset, Scrum is merely a framework that can use that mindset to get work done. Teams often struggle to get into the Agile mindset as it is very different from traditional project management approaches. The Scrum framework is a great way for teams to start practicing Agile principles and develop valuable products without confusion.

One of the greatest attributes of the Scrum framework is that it is easy for teams to adopt. The framework is based on gradual learning and adjusting to changing factors. Scrum assumes that a team is not experienced in the Agile way of thinking at the beginning of a project. It accommodates step-by-step learning for teams making it easy to adapt.

Furthermore, the Scrum framework is structured so that it enables teams to adjust to changing business environs and user requirements naturally. Re-prioritization is built into the Scrum process along with short cycles making it easier for teams to learn and improve in such business climates and projects.

Although structures, Scrum isn't too rigid, which is one of the key reasons behind its popularity. The Scrum framework can be tailored to the needs of a team, project, or company. Numerous successful Scrum theories exist when it comes to how teams can successfully adapt the Scrum framework, and any suitable combination of theories can be used as needed.

3.1 Scrum vs. Agile

Many individuals and even companies are confused when it comes to the relationship between Agile and Scrum. Some think that Scrum is a methodology just like Agile. Some believe that they are the same. While Agile and Scrum may be similar in many ways, they are not the same.

To put in the simplest terms, Agile is a methodology. The *Agile Manifesto* explains four core values and twelve guiding principles that can be used to help teams approach software development or the development of any other product differently to the sequential approach. Therefore, what the *Agile Manifesto* describes is a methodology and mindset or team.

When a team successfully adopts the values and principles of Agile, they can work productively and collaboratively to develop the product in small increments while increasing the product's value and dealing with changes through regular interactions with the customer. Agile simply provides guidelines on the mindset that can take teams there. However, Agile does not provide steps to achieve its values and principles.

Scrum, on the other hand, is a framework that helps teams adopt the Agile way of thinking and doing things. Scrum provides simple steps, which teams that do not have much or any prior Agile experience can follow to get into the Agile mindset. Therefore, teams use the Scrum framework to follow the Agile methodology.

Decision-making in Scrum is based on real-world outcomes instead of assumptions or speculations. Therefore, decisions can be easily justified, and they often tend to be the correct ones. Furthermore, there is very little disagreement or debate among team members regarding most decisions since they are based on real-world results.

Agile emphasizes the delivery of working increments of the product. Therefore, the development phase needs to be broken down into smaller cycles. However, there is no clear guideline about the exact or ideal duration of an iteration in the *Agile Manifesto*. However, in Scrum, the development phase is divided into short cycles known as sprints, which usually last for one or two weeks.

There is also very little uncertainty in the Scrum framework. All the defined roles, responsibilities, and meetings remain constant in Scrum. Therefore, Scrum enables teams to focus their energy and focus on the necessary unpredictability while reducing the unnecessary.

Going Agile as a team is difficult. It requires every team member to adopt and be in agreement about its values and principles. However, Scrum is a framework that incorporates Agile values and principles into a team so that it starts thinking and practicing the teachings of the *Agile Manifesto*.

Everyday communication. Short development cycles. Value to working product. Regular releases. Receiving regular feedback and embracing change. Continuous improvements through regularly reflecting on team performance. The framework makes Agile achievable for teams.

3.2 Scrum Roles

Scrum framework focuses on developing products incrementally with the use of small, self-organizing teams. A Scrum team should have more than three members and less than nine members according to the Scrum Guide. There are three key team roles in Scrum. They are the Scrum Master, Product Owner, and Development Team.

A Scrum team should be carefully put together to achieve the advantages offered by the Scrum framework. Scrum teams, much like Agile teams, should be cross-functional. It means that a Scrum team should consist of individuals of different skills and expertise who are required to develop the product without relying on anyone who does not belong to the team.

The team structure in the Scrum framework focuses on the development of small, self-organizing, and cross-functional teams that are flexible, creative, and productive. These independent teams are motivated by the trust that is put upon them to take ownership and get work done. They are trusted to the extent that they directly communicate with stakeholders for feedback.

The Scrum Master

The role responsible for guiding teams to implement the Scrum framework is called a Scrum Master. The Scrum framework is popular as a way to adopt the Agile way of thinking. However, teams require some knowledge and guidance to follow the Scrum framework. Some Scrum practices are often misunderstood and confused with others. Some individuals do not understand the purpose of certain Scrum values. The Scrum Master makes sure that everyone involved in a Scrum project, including the Product Owner, Development Team, and the stakeholders, abide by the Scrum theory, practices, rules, and values.

The Scrum Master plays the role of a servant-leader. The communication between the entities that do not belong to the Scrum team is left to the Scrum Master. The Scrum Master must ensure that interactions between such parties and the Scrum Team are productive and efficient. The Scrum Master is responsible for serving three entities: the company, Product Owner, and Development Team.

The Scrum Master serves the Product Owner by helping the Scrum Team understand the project scope, domain, and goals. He or she must help the Product Owner to manage the Product Backlog by recommending effective techniques. The Scrum Master also must ensure that the Product Owner is focused on maximizing the product's value with the way the Product Backlog is managed.

The Scrum Master must coach and guide the Development Team so that it is self-organizing and cross-functional. Any impediments against teamwork, productivity, efficiency, and Scrum practices need to be identified and eliminated by the Scrum Master. The Scrum Master also has to guide the Scrum Team, especially the Development Team, through Scrum Ceremonies, such as Sprint Planning, Daily Scrums, Sprint Reviews, and Sprint Retrospectives.

A company usually adopts the Scrum framework to develop value-added products while ensuring that projects do not run late or exceed budgets. It is also expected that implementing Scrum helps manage projects with changing requirements successfully. The Scrum Master must ensure that the company can adapt Scrum practices gradually without disrupting productivity and efficiency.

The Product Owner

Scrum is an Agile framework that enables teams to easily adapt to the Agile way of doing things without any prior experience and very little knowledge about the methodology. Therefore, the Product Owner in a Scrum team plays a very similar role that a Product Owner in an Agile environment does.

The Product Owner is responsible for the product's features that the Development Team complete incrementally so that the client can review *Done* versions of the product at the end of each Sprint. One of the Product Owner's key responsibilities is to maintain the Product Backlog. The Product Owner must prioritize items in the Product Backlog after consulting with the stakeholders so that the Development Team picks urgent tasks and features in Sprints instead of low-priority items.

The individuals who play the role of the Product Owner needs to negotiate what Product Backlog items will be completed in a given Sprint. The Development Team usually decides the number of tasks and which ones from the Product Backlog they will complete in a Sprint. The Product Owner can negotiate and agree with the Development Team to include or drop Product Backlog items from a Sprint.

The Product Owner is equal to any other role in a Scrum team in terms of rank. Many believe that the Product Owner plays a managing role; however, the role is intended to provide guidance to the product that is being developed by the Development Team. The Product Owner represents stakeholders within the Scrum team. Therefore, the stakeholders must respect the decisions that are made by the Product Owner during development.

The Development Team

The group of professionals trusted with the development of the product in a Scrum environment is the Development Team. Since Scrum teams are cross-functional, individuals with varying skill sets and expertise make up the Development Team to complete all aspects of the product development without relying on any external parties. For example, a Development Team that is developing software may include architects, software engineers, business analysts, and testers.

The Development Team collaboratively work on developing *Done* increments of the product until the end product is developed. The Development Team organizes itself. They determine the amount of work they are going to do in a Sprint and what tasks are completed during a Sprint.

The Product Owner can negotiate with the Development Team regarding the items or tasks that are chosen. However, the Product Owner cannot order the Development Team to include or exclude any tasks or items in a Sprint against their will.

The focus on the Development Team is to function efficiently and productively while maintaining a sustainable workload throughout the project. The members of the Development Team need to not only pull their weight but also support the team members since success in Scrum is measured by what the team achieves. As a result, every member of the Development Team is motivated to take ownership and pull their weight during a project.

There are no ranks, titles, or seniority within a Development Team. Every team member is treated equally irrespective of their experience, pay, and area of expertise. Such equality promotes teamwork and increases collaboration within the Development Team.

3.3 Scrum Ceremonies

Some of the key values and principles in the *Agile Manifesto* highlight the importance of face-to-face interactions or meetings between team members, stakeholders, and customers. Scrum is an Agile framework. It puts a similar focus on meetings to maintain efficient and clear communication during projects while avoiding time-consuming meetings and mediums.

Meetings in Scrum are known as *ceremonies*, and they are one of the most important elements of the framework. Scrum's time-boxed and iterative approach uses several ceremonies to maintain Agile practices throughout a project so that a highly satisfactory product is developed. These planned events also aim to increase regularity while reducing unplanned meetings that usually cost time and resources.

Furthermore, Scrum defines maximum durations for ceremonies within the framework. This encourages teams only to spend the prescribed amount of time for each ceremony to improve efficiency. Therefore, events in the Scrum framework have fixed durations depending on the team and the company. Each ceremony is also intended to help teams follow Agile values and principles.

What is a *Sprint* in Scrum?

It is safe to say that Sprints are the most important part of the Scrum framework. They are time-boxed events that should ideally last from one to four weeks. Therefore, a Sprint has a start date and an end date. The duration of a Sprint is determined by the team, depending on the nature of the product being developed. The duration of Sprints usually remains the same throughout a project.

If a complex product is being developed or the product requirements are likely to change quickly, it is recommended that Sprints should be one or two weeks long. If the product is less complex and unlikely to experience significant change, the Scrum team can opt for Sprints that are three to four weeks long.

Longer Sprints are not ideal since requirements can change during that time. The complexity of changes and risk can also change the longer a Sprint lasts. Therefore, according to Agile values and principles, it is better to make Sprints as short as possible.

One of the key advantages of Sprints is that they provide Scrum teams the opportunity to take a working product to a client for feedback. It ensures that the product they are developing is on track to be the best version of the final product. It also ensures that any changes the client might require can be completed as early as possible, as late changes usually cost more resources.

The end of a Sprint should see the release of a *Done* product increment. This version of the product must be used so that the customer can provide feedback regarding its features and request any changes as they see fit. The end of a Sprint marks the beginning of the next immediately.

A Sprint provides the Scrum team with goals that they work on achieving during the Sprint's length. The Scrum framework recommends that teams do not change the tasks that are agreed upon to be completed during a Sprint once it begins. Doing so usually adds more stress to the team while making it difficult for them to maintain quality. It may also contribute to sustainability issues in the long run, as teams are likely to burn out.

Most teams consider Sprints separate projects. If a Sprint lasts for two weeks, they look at it as a two-week-long project. During this time, several Scrum ceremonies are held. Some are held multiple times, while some only take place once during a specific stage of the

Sprint. These events are Sprint Planning, Daily Scum Stand-Ups, Sprint Reviews, and Sprint Retrospectives.

A Sprint may be canceled for a range of reasons. One of the most common reasons is the changing of requirements related to the tasks that have been selected for a Sprint. Changes in technology and the market can also result in the cancellation of Sprints.

Under such circumstances, completing those tasks serves no purpose toward the project. Therefore, the Sprint is canceled, and the team meets to plan a new one. The Product Owner usually decides whether to cancel a Sprint upon consulting the Scrum Master, the Scrum Team, and the stakeholders. If a Sprint is canceled, its goals or the Sprint Goal is considered as obsolete.

When a Sprint is canceled, the Product Backlog is thoroughly inspected to see if the work is releasable. The Product Owner will accept the work if it is releasable. Any incomplete items will be placed back on the Product Backlog to be selected in a future Sprint.

The Scrum framework recommends that Sprint cancellations be avoided. The cancellation of a Sprint usually results in wastage. It also costs additional resources to reassess and move on to a new Sprint. Scrum teams also find it challenging to regroup after the cancellation of a Sprint. As a result, Sprint cancellations are usually rare.

Sprint Planning

This Scrum ceremony takes place at the beginning of each Sprint with the Development Team, Scrum Master, and Product Owner in attendance. The Scrum framework prescribes a maximum duration of two hours for each week in a Sprint. Therefore, if the iteration is two weeks long, Sprint Planning should last four hours or less. If the iteration is for a month, Sprint planning should take a maximum of eight hours.

The Scrum Master has the responsibility to ensure that all the attendees fully understand the purpose of Sprint Planning so that the ceremony is highly productive. The Scrum Master must also ensure that the ceremony does not take longer than the prescribed time and that everything runs smoothly according to Scrum guidelines.

Sprint Planning discussions usually have two core topics. The first includes matters related to what the Development Team intends to complete during the next Sprint. The second includes matters on how the Development Team is going to achieve those goals.

Topic One: Defining Sprint Goals

Sprint Planning organizes the team's work for the next Sprint and sets it on a winning track from the outset. The Product Owner comes into the meeting with a prioritized Product Backlog. These items are then discussed with the Development Team. The Development Team will forecast the amount of work from the Product Backlog that they will sustainably and qualitatively complete. The effort that is required to complete Product Backlog items is estimated collectively by the entire group.

Important factors such as past Sprint performances, the sustainable capacity of the Development Team, and the most recent increment are considered when selecting items from the Product Backlog for the next Sprint. The Development Team needs to take in as much work as possible while committing to completing the work by the Sprint's scheduled end date. They must carefully consider the workload since it is highly prescribed that the workload can be sustained throughout the project without team members burning out.

The Product Owner sometimes converses with the Development Team to make trade-offs. If agreed, certain items that are in the Sprint Backlog are transferred back to the Product Backlog with the agreed Product Backlog items coming into the Sprint Backlog. Therefore, the discussions between the Product Owner and the Development Team can often feel like negotiations.

Topic Two: How to Achieve the Sprint Goals

Once the Scrum Team agrees on *what* they are going to complete in the next Sprint, *how* they will achieve those Sprint Goals is discussed. The items that were agreed to be completed by the

Development Team are now transferred to the Sprint Backlog. All the items in the Sprint Backlog need to be completed to a *Done* state by the end of the Sprint.

Discussions regarding how each Sprint Backlog item is going to be completed to a *Done* state are then discussed. The team also draws a plan for the next few days while deciding which Sprint Backlog items will be prioritized. The Product Owner participates in these discussions to provide clarity regarding the backlog items that are being discussed.

There is a likelihood of the Development Team, realizing that they can do more work during the Sprint after these discussions. In such a scenario, the remaining Product Backlog items are discussed and added to the Sprint Backlog. The team then moves on to determining how those items are going to be completed. Upon agreement, the meeting is adjourned, and the agreed Product Backlog items become the Sprint Backlog.

Sprint Goal

One or a collection of objectives for a given Sprint is known as the Sprint Goal. The Sprint Goal should provide some guidance regarding the *Done* increment of the product that will be released at the end of the Sprint. Completion of items that are transferred from the Product Backlog to the Sprint Backlog should allow the Scrum Team to achieve the Sprint Goal. The Scrum Team should identify the Sprint Goal during Sprint Planning so that it motivates them and provides necessary guidance throughout the Sprint.

The Sprint Goal provides the Development Team with an idea regarding the *Done* increment that they are working toward. Therefore, the Sprint Goal keeps the Development Team on track towards completing a successful Sprint. If the Sprint Backlog items are different from the Sprint Goal or do not allow the Development Team to achieve the Sprint Goal, they are renegotiated, and suitable items are added to the Sprint Goal after negotiating with the Product Owner.

For example, if the Sprint Goal is to create the shopping cart of a website. The Sprint Backlog should include items that are related to the shopping cart feature. However, if the Sprint Backlog has items that do not contribute to the completion of the shopping cart, the Development Team needs to renegotiate and transfer Product Backlog items that are related to the shopping cart feature into the Sprint Backlog.

Daily Scrum

Stand-up meetings that take place daily with the attendance of the Product Owner, Scrum Master and the Development Team are known as Daily Scrums. It is recommended that Daily Scrums are held before starting work for the day. Therefore, they usually fall in the mornings unless team members are located in different time zones.

Scrum recommends that Daily Scrums are held while standing up. Sitting down is discouraged since it makes attendees comfortable, which usually results in meetings running longer than required. A Daily Scrum should not last longer than fifteen minutes. It is also customary to hold Daily Scrums at the same location at the same time to maintain continuity.

One of the main purposes of Daily Scrums is to enhance communication, performance, and collaboration among the Development Team. The Development Team answers three main questions during a Daily Scrum: "What did I achieve yesterday?", "What will I work on today?" and "Is there anything stopping me from achieving it?"

The first question takes a look at the previous day while providing the Development Team a view of where they stand in terms of the Sprint Goal. Doing so provides the team with an understanding of what needs to be done to keep on track regarding achieving their goals as a team.

Then the team focuses on what tasks they are going to complete that day. Work is divided among team members as equally as possible. Such self-organizing teams often take more ownership of their work that results in better productivity and efficiency. Any factors that block team members from achieving their daily goals are also discussed at the Daily Scrum.

Teams work collaboratively to find solutions for such obstacles. If any team member needs help, the Development Team usually discusses ways to provide the necessary help. For example, if David needs to finish his work for John to start working on his task, the team may divide both the tasks among David and John or assign a different task for John.

Daily Scrums are usually informal. The way they are held depends on the Development Team. Some teams use discussions while others use questions. It is up to the team to decide how they are going to hold Daily Scrums.

Different team members typically meet after the conclusion of a Daily Scrum to further plan their work since some team members may be working on the same tasks or ones that are connected to each other. The Scrum Master guides the team during Daily Scrums and makes sure that they do not last longer than fifteen minutes. The Scrum Master must also ensure that the Development Team is not interrupted by any others during Daily Scrums even if they are invited to the Development Team meeting.

Sprint Review

The end of a Sprint should see the Scrum Team presenting a *Done* increment of the product to the customer. This occurs during the Sprint Review, where the Development Team, Scrum Master, Product Owner, and the project stakeholders are present. The Product Owner is responsible for inviting the necessary stakeholders to a Sprint Review.

A Sprint Review should ideally last an hour or less for a Sprint that spans a week. The Scrum Master has to ensure that the ceremony does not last longer than ideal. The Scrum Master must also ensure that the purpose of the Sprint Review is understood by everyone present.

The Development Team presents what was achieved during the recent Sprint by showcasing the product's *Done* increment. The project stakeholders, along with the Product Owner, inspect the product increment, and look for any deviations from the Product Backlog items. If any such deviations are identified, changes are requested. The stakeholders can also request changes if original changes have been changed or if they find new ways to add value to the end product.

Many Scrum Teams and stakeholders confuse Sprint Reviews with traditional Status Meetings. Sprint Reviews compared to Status Meetings are highly informal. The emphasis is more on receiving feedback from the stakeholders rather than presenting the project's state and progress. However, the presentation is done so that the stakeholders can provide feedback.

During the Sprint Review, the Product Owner informally lets the attendees know the Product Backlog items that were completed in the Sprint. Then the Development Team lets the attendees know how the Sprint progressed, including the problems that came up and how they solved them.

Then the Development Team presents the product's *Done* increment to the attendees. For example, if the Shopping Cart feature was added to the website, which is the end product of the project, the Development Team will present the *Done* Shopping Cart feature to the attendees.

The stakeholders and the Product Owner may see that the Development Team has not developed the Shopping Cart Summary at the check-out during the presentation. They may request it to be added. Furthermore, the stakeholders may say that they would like to display a new type of tax in the Shopping Card Summary, which may not be a requirement that was captured earlier. Both changes will make it into the Product Backlog.

Therefore, the Product Backlog is likely to be changed during a Sprint Review or as a result of it, with items being added or removed by the Product Owner. The Sprint Review, as a result, should provide the attendees, especially the stakeholders, with an update regarding the project timeline, budget, and the capabilities of the end product.

Sprint Retrospective

Scrum, being an Agile framework, encourages teams to improve as they move from one development cycle to another. Sprints provide teams opportunities to improve both as teams as well as individuals. The Scrum ceremonies that provide teams the opportunity to reflect on their work and improve are known as Sprint Retrospectives.

The Sprint Retrospectives usually take place after the conclusion of the Sprint Review. It is also customary for the Sprint Planning to begin once the Sprint Retrospective is over. A Sprint Retrospective should be no longer than 45 minutes for a week-long Sprint. Similarly, it must not exceed three hours for a Sprint of four weeks. The Scrum Master guides Sprint Retrospectives and ensures that they do not exceed the optimal allocated duration.

Sprint Retrospectives are attended by the Scrum Master, Development Team, and the Product Owner. The Scrum Master must ensure that all attendees understand the aim of Sprint Retrospectives and that the ceremony is productive. It is also important to highlight that the Scrum Master's role is equal to everyone else in the ceremony; however, he or she guides the ceremony.

Sprint Retrospectives are ceremonies that enable teams to reflect on how development went during a Sprint. Individual performances, as well as tools and processes, are openly discussed so that teams can come up with solutions to avoid the repetition of mistakes and improve. The Scrum Team's collaborative performance is also reflected upon at Sprint Retrospectives. Any solutions that are identified will be practiced and applied in the next Sprint.

The Scrum framework recommends that the Scrum Master provides the team with motivation and encouragement to improve continuously so that the next Sprints and future projects run smoothly.

A Sprint Retrospective is adjourned once the team has identified what went wrong and what they will do in the next Sprint to overcome those struggles. However, it is up to the team to decide when and if they are going to implement the solutions identified at a Sprint Retrospective since the ceremony only aims to provide them with an opportunity to reflect and improve.

3.4 Scrum Artifacts

One of the biggest downfalls of traditional project management was the heavy focus on documentation. Agile emerged to reduce documentation; however, some documentation was still recommended to keep teams and stakeholders informed and aligned. Scrum, being an Agile framework, involves less documentation. The documents that aid the management of product development in Scrum are known as Scrum Artifacts.

Product Backlog

This document is a list that includes all the requirements and features of the end product. The Product Backlog items are prioritized so that they can be selected into Sprints accordingly by the Development Team. The Product Owner is responsible for the creation and maintenance of the Product Backlog.

One of the Product Backlog's unique features is that it remains a *work in progress* until the end of the project. The Scrum framework embraces change. Therefore, any changes identified by the Scrum Team or stakeholders are added to the Product Backlog by the Product Owner. Then the list is ordered again.

It is natural for the Product Backlog to be simple at the start of a project. It may only include requirements and features for a basic product. However, the Product Backlog evolves parallel to the product's development. New features, functionalities, requirements, enhancements, and fixes are added to the list along the way, while some items may also be taken down.

For example, when it comes to the development of a website, the Product Backlog may only include the development of the website's basic elements. The completion of the first couple of Sprints may see the Product Backlog being populated with more complex requirements, such as the product and category pages.

Each item listed on the Product Backlog needs to have a description, order, estimate, and value. These include the descriptions that are intended to aid testing. These items may be updated or removed as the product is developed, and feedback is received from the stakeholders.

Some companies may consist of multiple Scrum teams working on the same product. Although multiple products collaboratively develop the same product, only one Product Backlog is maintained. However, items may be grouped so that teams can easily identify the items assigned to their teams.

One of the most important activities involving the Product Backlog is Product Backlog refinement. The Product Owner, along with the Development Team, adds descriptions, priority levels, and estimates to the Product Backlog items. The refinement of the Product Backlog is an ongoing activity where Scrum Teams collectively decide when to do it.

The Scrum Guide prescribes that less than ten percent of the Development Team's capacity should be consumed for Product Backlog refinement. However, the Product Owner can update the Product Backlog and its items at any time. Product Backlog refinement is important since the Scrum Team uses the Product Backlog to understand the end product that is being developed.

Furthermore, the Product Backlog is used to weigh the work that needs to be done to reach the project's end goal. The Product Owner maintains the Product Backlog by keeping track of the work completed and the work that remains. These updates usually take place during Sprint Reviews.

Agile methodology and the Scrum framework both measure progress by the work that has been completed. Therefore, progress is determined by comparing the amount of work that remains between each Sprint. For example, if 500 hours' worth of work remained at the end of the previous Sprint and only 450 hours remain by the end of the current Sprint, the Scrum Team can say that the current Sprint achieved 50 hours' worth of work.

The amount of work that needs to be completed to close the project is calculated similarly using the Product Backlog. Therefore, the Product Backlog acts as a valuable and key Scrum Artifact for the Scrum Team as well as the stakeholders.

Sprint Backlog

The Product Backlog items that the Development Team chooses to complete in a Sprint are populated on the Sprint Backlog. The Sprint Backlog works as a guide for the Scrum Team to achieve the Sprint Goal and release a *Done* product increment at the end of the Sprint. Therefore, the Sprint Backlog can be seen as a forecast of the product increment created by the Development Team, detailing what will be completed in the Sprint and the amount of work that needs to be done to achieve it.

The Development Team uses the Sprint Backlog to guide Daily Scrums. The team discusses the current state of work by assessing the work completed on the previous day and proceeds to make plans for the day. They use the Sprint Backlog to be reminded of the work left to do by the end of the Sprint.

The Sprint Backlog is a *work in progress* similar to the Product Backlog. However, it is the Development Team that modifies the Sprint Backlog. Any new items added as a result of changes are added to the Sprint Backlog by the Development Team. Estimates of the work that needs to be done are updated on the Sprint Backlog every day so that the team is aware of the progress they are making toward achieving the Sprint Goal.

The Development Team can remove any items in the Sprint Backlog that they feel are unnecessary. The Sprint Backlog is a

Scrum Artifact that belongs to the Development Team. It is often used by teams to guide them toward achieving Sprint Goals without missing any Product Backlog items that are chosen to be completed in a Sprint.

3.5 A Scrum Example

Peter is assigned to the role of Product Owner of a project that intends to develop a software application. Peter starts his work by gathering requirements and writing down use cases upon having discussions with the customer, other stakeholders, and the architects. Peter goes on to create the Product Backlog for the project after he completes collecting requirements and high-level uses cases.

Peter seeks a few senior developers' help when creating the Product Backlog, especially with prioritizing items and making estimations. At the end of the session, Peter completes the Product Backlog with all the gathered requirements and use cases along with their priorities and estimations.

Now that the high-level use cases have been listed on the Product Backlog and prioritized, Peter begins to break them down into smaller user stories. Once he has broken down enough high-level user stories, he informs the Scrum Master for the first Sprint Planning ceremony.

John, who is the Scrum Master, informs the Development Team regarding the Sprint Planning ceremony. Peter briefs the Development Team regarding the project and goes on to present Product Backlog items starting with the highest priority to the lowest. Then, the Development Team members ask Peter some questions regarding certain Product Backlog items that Peter clarifies.

The Development Team discusses their capacity and whether they have the required expertise to complete the project. After agreeing that they have the experts in the team, and confirming the amount of work they can complete during the Sprint, the Development Team commits to complete Product Backlog stories 1,

3, 4, 5, 7, and 8. Items 2 and 6 are not chosen since they have some technical requirements that are not yet in place. John goes on to adjourn the Sprint Planning ceremony.

Once the Sprint Planning meeting is over, John asks the Development Team to explain how they intend to complete the items that they committed to. The Development Team creates a task board that acts as a Sprint Backlog. Different team members are assigned to complete tasks that are on the board. No other Scrum ceremonies occur for the remainder of the day with the Development Team carrying out their work.

The next day starts with the Scrum Master, John, calling the first Daily Scrum meeting. John asks each individual of the Development Team to let everyone know what they have achieved so far. As each team member provides information about the work that is being achieved, John updates the Task Board with estimations of the remaining hours for each task.

John then asks team members about what they plan on doing for the day. He also asks if any obstacles might keep them from doing their work. Team members briefly explain what they intend to achieve during the day. Most team members do not have any impediments against achieving their goals except for Ross, who seems to have a license issue with one of the software tools he is using.

John asks if any other members of the Development Team have the same issue. Upon checking, he finds out that Molly also has the same issue. John tells them that he will look into the matter. The Daily Scrum is adjourned and only takes thirteen minutes.

John calls the systems administrator and informs him about the license issue Ross and Molly are facing. The systems administrator attends to the problem quickly by purchasing two licenses for them. Upon hearing that the license issue has been sorted out, John checks with Ross and Molly to see if they can work without any issues.

The next day begins with the entire Scrum Team getting together for the Daily Scrum. The meeting progresses well with team members providing updates regarding the work that was achieved the previous day, their plans for the next day, and John updating the Task Board. This Daily Scrum only takes ten minutes.

In a few hours, Kenny is faced with a problem regarding one of the user stories. He heads over to Peter, who is the Product Owner, to ask for clarification. Peter explains the user story to Kenny, who finds the clarity he was looking for. He can carry on with his work without any problems.

The remaining ten days of the two-week Sprint progress without any major incidents. Daily Scrums take place with the Scrum Team being updated regarding the progress of the work.

On the final day of the first Sprint, John calls for a Sprint Review meeting. John also invites Brenda, who represents the customer for the meeting. The Development Team has already prepared a computer with the *Done* product increment to be presented at the meeting. The latest release is presented to the attendees.

Peter, along with Brenda, follows the presentation very carefully, with Peter concluding that the Product Backlog items 1, 4, 5, and 7 have been completed. However, item 3 was not completed on time. Therefore, it was not included in the product increment that was presented.

Furthermore, item 8 needs to be clarified as it is missing some points. Brenda points out that item 5 needs to be slightly changed with Peter taking note. The Sprint Review meeting is adjourned.

John calls for the Sprint Retrospective ceremony a while later, where the team discusses things that went well and what did not during the Sprint. The reasons behind item 3 not being completed are looked into with the team discussing ways to avoid similar mistakes in the future. The reasons behind the team's failure to identify the missing points in item 8 are discussed.

The Development Team mentions that one of the main reasons behind the few downfalls in the first Sprint was due to the lack of understanding of the system architecture. John asks Peter to address this issue. Peter responds by inviting a system architect to take the

Development Team through the system architecture. The Sprint Retrospective is adjourned with the team having identified ways to improve. Peter updates the Product Backlog with new items that he gathered after having a discussion with Brenda. Furthermore, he adds the missing points of the user story 8 and updates the Product Backlog. He also adds the changes Brenda requested to item 5.

Peter calls for the Sprint Planning meeting in the morning on the next day. The Development Team discusses user stories with Peter and commits to some under the guidance of John. The Sprint Planning meeting is adjourned, and the second Sprint begins. The Daily Scrums take place for the next fourteen days. The items that the team committed to are completed without any issues.

At the Sprint Review, Brenda requests a few changes, which are updated on the Product Backlog by Peter. The Sprint Retrospective also concludes with the team hoping to make some minor improvements. Peter calls for the Sprint Planning meeting for the third and final Sprint on the same day. The Development Team decides to complete all the remaining Product Backlog items in this Sprint and commits to them.

The Sprint runs smoothly, with the team functioning well. Daily Scrums take place efficiently with John's direction, while Peter is involved whenever the Development Team requires any clarifications. The third and final Sprint ends with the Development Team completing all the committed tasks successfully.

The final product is presented at the Sprint Review. The customer, Brenda, and the Product Owner, Peter, are highly satisfied with the end product. John calls for the Sprint Retrospective to finally identify the lessons that can be learned from the final Sprint. The project is closed.

Chapter 4: Kanban Method

Kanban, which is spelled "Kamban" in Japanese, is an Agile framework that uses visualization to understand processes and workflows better and actual work done in those processes. Kanban has become popular to identify and manage bottlenecks in workflows so that the work runs smoothly at an optimal speed.

Kamban, in Japanese, means "Billboard," and in Chinese, it means "Signboard." These visual representations are used to indicate the "available capacity to work." Therefore, Kanban is a framework that helps manage processes and workflows by visualizing work. It ultimately helps processes achieve optimal efficiency and adapt to the Agile way of thinking.

Although Kanban is a framework that originated in the manufacturing industry, it became highly popular in the software development world. It has since been used across sectors, especially in the recent past. However, there are many misinterpretations about Kanban as it gains in popularity. Therefore, it is important to understand Kanban correctly before implementing the framework.

4.1 Kanban and Agile

Agile is a project management methodology that can be considered a way of thinking, where projects are broken into more manageable smaller chunks. Highly motivated, self-organizing teams work on those chunks to deliver working increments of the product to receive feedback from the stakeholders along the way. Teams in Agile environments regularly and continuously improve. Agile methodology was first intended to be used in the software development industry; however, it has been adopted by many other industries to manage complex projects with changing requirements.

Kanban, on the other hand, is a method or a framework that agrees with the Agile values and principles. Many companies find Agile somewhat difficult to adopt since it requires coaching and guidance from someone who has knowledge and experience about the methodology. However, Kanban is similar to the Scrum framework as it enables companies to become Agile without requiring much experience and know-how.

Therefore, Kanban can be called an Agile framework. It has many similarities to Scrum, as well as subtle differences. More importantly, Kanban's core philosophy is similar to the Agile way of thinking, just like Scrum. Scrum and Kanban use the visual representation of work by using a physical board or a digital representation of a Kanban board. The work in a Kanban or Scrum project can be divided into three main categories: the work that needs to be done, work in progress, and the work that has been achieved.

The Kanban method is based on the *Kanban Board*, which plays a vital role in helping teams visualize the workflow and progress toward their ultimate goals. Teams can easily understand how different teams complete tasks while they collaborate with the same outcome. Every piece of work at varying development stages are represented on the Kanban Board.

The visual representation of tasks and how they are achieved not only bring transparency and clarity into teams but also helps them identify and manage bottlenecks that they may never have identified. The Kanban method also allows teams to reprioritize work according to their stakeholders' needs, resulting in increased customer satisfaction. Teams are also encouraged to collaborate and strive for improvements by solving weaknesses in their processes.

The Kanban method allows more flexibility when it comes to the tasks that are selected to be completed in an iteration. For example, Kanban does not have a Sprint backlog where only the tasks that are in the Sprint Backlog are completed in a Sprint. Therefore, teams implementing Kanban can work on tasks if they become more urgent while in the middle of a development cycle.

The Kanban method was first applied in software development by David J. Anderson in 2004, almost half a century since its inception in Japan. David was inspired by the works of Taiichi Ohno, Edward Demmings, Eli Goldratt, and many others. He published *Kanban: Successful Evolutionary Change for Your Technology Business* in 2010, which is considered one of the most comprehensive guides to the Kanban Method.

Kanban soon started expanding into other industries. Its focus on gradual improvements within teams that were along the Agile way of thinking was one of the key factors behind its popularity. Kanban is now used in many industries and sectors, including information technology, sales and marketing, recruitment, staffing, and procurement. The principles of the Kanban Method are also so simple and powerful that they could be applied to any business function.

4.2 The Origins of Kanban

The Kanban method goes back decades; however, it is just starting to gain popularity in some industries. The Japanese carmaker, Toyota, stared optimizing and enhancing their processes using a similar model to what was used to stack shelves in supermarkets. The model is based on stocking a similar number of products on the shelves according to consumer demand.

The practice was proven to be successful since inventory levels matched the patterns around consumption. Therefore, supermarkets found it easier to manage inventory. More importantly, they managed to reduce excess stock in their stores that they were responsible for. However, any given product was still available for the customers whenever they needed it.

In the early 1940s, Toyota was not happy with the level of efficiency and productivity in their firms, especially compared to their American rivals. Taiichi Ohno, who was a businessman and industrial engineer at Toyota in Japan, came up with a very simple planning system. The system aimed to control and manage inventory and work at every stage of production.

The system was called Kanban. By implementing Kanban, Toyota managed to increase productivity and reduce costs related to maintaining inventories of raw materials, semi-finished, and finished products. Kanban controls the flow of the product from the supplier to the consumer. As a result, it can help eliminate many costly issues, such as the disruption of the supply and the overstocking of materials and goods during manufacturing.

One of the basic requirements of Kanban is continuous monitoring. Any process that implements Kanban needs to be monitored closely and continuously for it to be successful. Attention must be given to identify and avoid bottlenecks that can potentially disrupt the production process.

Before the application of Kanban, Toyota was dealing with massive overheads relating to inventory levels. There was no systematic relationship with their inventory levels and the requirement of those materials for production. Kanban introduced a visual approach to overcome such struggles where capacity levels in the factory were communicated using Kanban cards.

When a production line in the factory ran out of nuts and bolts, a Kanban was sent to the warehouse with a description of the material needed, the amount needed, and other important details. The warehouse would then issue the exact number of nuts and bolts to the factory line while sending a Kanban to their supplier for the same material and the same amount. Upon receiving the Kanban, the supplier would issue the materials to the warehouse from the stocks.

The Kanban system eliminates the need for the factory floor, warehouse, and the supplier to maintain too much inventory. They only need to maintain just enough to keep production going. Whenever they issue a certain item, a Kanban is sent out requesting for the same amount so that the optimal inventory levels can be maintained to keep production flowing.

4.3 Key Values and Philosophies of Kanban

The Kanban Method prescribes several practices and principles that can be applied to teams to improve their workflow. It is popular for being a highly non-disruptive method to encourage continuous and regular improvements to processes. Kanban principles and practices help businesses achieve better flow in their processes, reduced cycle times, increased predictability, and increased product value. Therefore, adopting the Kanban method is a highly attractive proposition for many businesses belonging to different sectors.

Kanban Principles

The Kanban Method describes several principles that can be easily practiced by individuals and teams to enjoy the benefits that the method offers. These principles are very simple and easy to understand. Furthermore, they are usually unlikely to disrupt a process, making them very easy to adopt.

Start with What You Are Doing Now

Kanban recommends that companies not disrupt the way things are done when adopting the method. The method sees such disruption as negative and disadvantageous. The current processes should be left alone while Kanban is applied directly to the workflow. Changes to the processes can be done gradually at a pace that teams are comfortable with.

Agree to Pursue Incremental and Evolutionary Change

Making radical changes to a team's process often reduces productivity for a considerable amount of time. As a result, Kanban recommends making smaller incremental changes. The application of radical changes often leads to resistance from teams and employees, resulting in the entire exercise being unsuccessful.

Initially, Respect Current Roles, Job Titles, and Responsibilities

Methodologies such as Agile and frameworks such as Scrum impose organizational changes and changes to the way employees are managed. As a result, many companies struggle to adopt such methodologies and frameworks. Kanban is easy to implement since it does not require any organizational changes.

Existing roles, responsibilities, and the way employees function in their roles are left alone. Therefore, factors that contribute to good performances are left alone. The implementation of Kanban will result in team members implementing required changes without the need to enforce them.

Encourage Acts of Leadership at All Levels

Kanban, being an Agile method, encourages teams to improve continuously. The Kanban method does not limit leadership qualities to specific job titles or roles. One does not need to have seniority or a management role to become a leader when Kanban is applied. Team members at all levels are encouraged to share their ideas so that teams can collaboratively improve as they progress with work.

4.4 The Goal of Kanban

The Kanban Method is a non-disruptive management system that enables processes to be improved using small steps instead of radical changes. Many minor changes are used to improve processes without risking the current processes and causing teams and stakeholders to resist change. Principles and practices in Kanban aim to achieve a set of goals that are highly beneficial for companies.

Planning Flexibility

A Kanban team focuses on the work at hand. They do not commit to new work until the work in progress is completed. As soon as a work in progress task is completed, the item at the top of the backlog is attended to. The Product Owner maintains backlog priority, and any changes to its priority do not affect the work that is in progress.

As long as high priority items are accurately identified, the team automatically ends up committing to them. This results in teams offering maximum value to the company without limiting them to iterations. Iterations often limit teams to a number of tasks that they commit to at the very beginning of it.

For example, a Scrum team commits to several tasks from the Product Backlog to be completed during the Sprint. These items are then added to the Sprint Backlog. The team does not commit to any more items during the Sprint. However, a Kanban team does not limit itself to a certain list of items. Instead, it focuses on finishing the work at hand. As soon as the work is complete, the task with the highest priority is taken from the Product Backlog. Therefore, the Kanban Method offers better flexibility when it comes to planning.

Shorter Time Cycles

One of the key metrics for Kanban teams is Cycle Time. It refers to the time that a unit of work takes to travel from the moment the development starts until it is shipped out. Optimizing cycle time makes the team more productive and enables them to forecast how quickly products can be delivered correctly. The Kanban Method aims to shorten cycle time by overlapping skill sets through mentoring and knowledge transfers.

Reducing Bottlenecks

The more items that are in progress, the more teams need to multi-task, and the longer it takes for those items to be completed. As a result, the Kanban Method focuses on limiting the work that is in progress. Work in Progress Limits can be used to highlight bottlenecks within a process as well as backups that are usually caused by a lack of people and skillsets.

Visual Metrics

One of the Kanban Method's core values is to continuously strive for improvements so that teams become increasingly efficient and effective. Teams respond well to visual metrics, such as charts, where they can see improvements visually and become motivated. Kanban teams use cumulative flow charts and control charts as visual metrics to identify and eliminate bottlenecks, resulting in improved processes.

Continuous Delivery

The Kanban Method focuses on continuously delivering working increments of a developed product. For example, when a Kanban team is developing the software, they are focused on building code for a particular item, testing the code, and releasing the item once it is done so that the customer can use the feature and provide feedback.

4.5 Implementing Kanban

The Kanban method has gained popularity across various sectors as it is easy to apply to processes and setups. It clearly describes what needs to be done to avoid disruptions to processes and cause resistance within teams. The six core practices explained in Kanban are aimed toward the implementation of Kanban successfully without inducing negative resistance disrupting the performance of teams.

The Kanban Method aims to increase project performance by visualizing the workflow while encouraging teams to improve continuously. It also enables the customer to be more involved during the development phase of a project, just like other Agile frameworks. However, Kanban also has some features that are different from many Agile frameworks.

Most Agile frameworks feature iterations that last a certain period and involve multiple tasks. However, a development cycle in Kanban is the time taken for a single user story to go through all the stages of work in a process until it is marked as *Done*. Therefore, implementing the Kanban method can be tricky for some companies. Patience and gradual changes may be required when implementing the Kanban method.

Step 1: Visualize the Flow of Work

The first fundamental step toward adopting the Kanban Method is to visualize the steps in the process currently being used to develop a product or service in a company. Visualization of the steps can be done physically, with the use of a Kanban Board, or digitally, with the use of a digital tool that represents a Kanban Board. Kanban Boards representing different processes can look different. Some may look simple, while others may be very complex, depending on the processes that they represent.

Different types of cards and colors can be used to highlight the significance of different work items. Kanban Boards also feature Swim Lanes, where each lane is dedicated to a particular type of work item. However, the Kanban Method recommends that things be kept simple initially while focusing on gradual changes. Therefore, a single Swim Lane may represent the entire process in the beginning with the possibility of gradual redesigning of the representation down the road as teams become more comfortable with the visualization of the processes.

Step 2: Limiting *Work in Progress* (WIP)

This practice encourages teams to finish the tasks that are at hand or *in progress* before committing to new ones. Therefore, the work that is currently marked as *Work in Progress* first needs to be completed and marked as *Done* before taking up new work. This practice results in the efficient use of the capacity within teams. They end up completing work and taking up more work at a faster pace.

It is natural for teams to struggle when it comes to initially determining their WIP limits. Therefore, it is recommended that Kanban is implemented with no WIP limits in place. The work in progress is first observed, and limits are only applied after analyzing substantial data. Most teams typically start with a Work in Progress Limit of between one to 1.5 times the number of team members contributing to a specific stage. Introducing WIP limits to columns in the Kanban Board helps team members finish what they have at hand first before committing to new work. Furthermore, it also provides transparency—since stakeholders, including the customer, can see that the team's capacity is limited. This encourages them to plan their requests and manage their expectations.

Step 3: Managing Flow

Once the first two practices are implemented, managing and improving the flow begins. It is a difficult practice to implement, and it must also be done carefully. Now that the workflow has been defined and Work in Progress Limits have been carefully set, there should be a smooth flow within those WIP limits or work should start piling up. The workflow needs to be adjusted so that it is improved, depending on how it flows upon applying the first two principles.

One of the key ways of achieving this goal is by carefully observing the workflow to identify bottlenecks. Attention must be given to intermediate wait stages where work items that are marked as *Done* are handed off. Reducing the time that *Done* items are parked in these intermediate work stages results in eliminating bottlenecks and reducing cycle time.

As improvements are made gradually, teams begin to deliver work smoothly and more predictably. When predictability improves, it is easier to make commitments to customers and their requests without taking the risk of disappointing them. Improving the accuracy of forecasts regarding product completion times is one of the main advantages that the Kanban method offers.

Step 4: Making Process Policies Explicit

Just like processes are visualized explicitly, the Kanban Method recommends that policies or rules and guidelines are made explicit. These policies decide the way teams work, and making rules and guidelines overtly encourages everyone who takes part in those processes to work the same way. They will know how to work in any situation according to the rules and guidelines that are made very clear.

Processes may have different policies at different levels or stages. They may exist in specific Swim Lanes or specific columns. They may involve a checklist that dictates entry or exit criteria for a certain column. Making policies unambiguous helps processes run smoothly without irregularities. Therefore, policies need to be made explicit and represented visually on the Kanban Board for each Swim Lane and column.

Step 5: Implementing Feedback Loops

Any good methodology, framework, or system emphasizes feedback loops. The Kanban Method helps organizations implement different kinds of feedback loops. These include reviewing different stages in the workflow, reports, and metrics, as well as visual clues that provide feedback regarding the workflow that needs to be implemented. Feedback needs to be taken early, especially when things are not going great, so improvements can be made. Feedback loops are critical to make those improvements and deliver a satisfactory product or service to the customer.

Step 6: Improving Collaboratively and Evolving Experimentally by Using the Scientific Method

The Kanban Method enables companies to gradually improve their processes and workflows without posing difficulties to those involved in the processes. The use of the scientific method is encouraged to make those improvements and evolve through experimentation. A hypothesis is first formed, followed by tests. Changes are then made according to the outcomes of those tests.

When the Kanban Method is implemented, there needs to be continuous evaluations and improvements based on those evaluations. The Kanban system makes it easy to experiment since it provides signals to help teams figure out if a change is helping them improve.

Chapter 5: Lean Thinking

Most companies that have been in operation for a few decades or even more still run with the same processes and setups that were put in place decades ago. Some processes may have been left untouched since the company started operations. Many business owners believe that they can use the same process over decades simply because they work. It may look true and practiced at a glance. After all, why fix something that is not broken?

However, the problem with such an approach toward using the same decades-long processes is that the world of business is continuously evolving. There may be rare instances where leaving processes as they are is the wisest choice. However, generally, most businesses need to evolve with the world that they belong to.

Take the hospitality industry, for example. People may have checked-in casually to a hotel at the front desk where all the gathering of details, payments, security deposits, customer reviews, and complaints may have been carried out. The front desk handled all those tasks decades ago. Today, the front desk is still capable of handling all those tasks. It can even handle a range of tasks much quicker compared to those days. However, most of those tasks do not make it to the front desk.

Most customers search for hotels over the Internet. They may provide some or most of their details when making a reservation, and they may also pay in advance electronically. Most customers will leave reviews and complaints online after their stay. Therefore, the front desk has become less important; however, it can get things done just as it did decades ago.

Imagine if a hotel decided to solely rely on the "front days" like the good old days just because it works. Imagine a hotel not providing online reservations, payments, reviews, and complaints in modern times. The chances are that most guests will not even know about the hotel.

Therefore, most businesses need to evolve alongside the world, industry, technology, and consumer behavior to remain successful. Competition keeps increasing, and newer players enter markets with innovative solutions. The businesses that have been around for a long time need to continuously challenge themselves to improve and fine-tune their processes.

Lean Management focuses on reducing and eliminating waste. Various industries have used the teachings and philosophies of Lean starting from the manufacturing industry and going as far as the software development industry. Companies have been able to increase productivity, eliminate waste, and improve quality using Lean Management. However, the business world is still discovering the true value and power of Lean Thinking and Lean Management.

Lean Management reduces waste and focuses on adding value to products and services that are being developed. Therefore, Lean is a set of tools and techniques that can be used to reduce waste and add value to different processes. However, it must be noted that the definition of Lean may slightly vary depending on the industry, country, region, or even the company it is implemented in. For example, Lean is considered a mindset or a way of thinking instead of a set of tools and techniques.

History of Lean

When it comes to the origins of Lean, Toyota rings bells in many people's minds. However, it must be noted that the roots of Lean Thinking go back to fifteenth-century Venice. The concept of Lean was successfully used in manufacturing by Henry Fort in 1799. The groundbreaking concept of interchangeable parts was also introduced by Eli Whitney the same year.

In 1913, Henry Ford came up with an idea to experiment with the flow of production in the application of interchanging parts. The purpose was to standardize work. However, Ford's system was limited in use since it lacked variety. It was only applicable to one specification. Nevertheless, an important stride was made.

Shiego Shingo and Taiichi Ohno, working for Toyota, invented the Toyota Production System in the 1930s. Shiego Shingo and Taiichi Ohno were inspired by Henry Ford's theory relating to the flow of production. Toyota's systems aimed to reduce the cost of production, improve the quality of products, and enhance the throughput times to meet dynamic customer requirements.

John Krafcik first introduced the term "Lean" in one of his articles in 1988, titled "Triumph of the Lean Production System." The article explained how Lean manufacturing was used in various plants to achieve higher quality and productivity levels compared to traditional manufacturing processes.

He also highlighted that the technology that was being used in different plants did not affect performance levels. Furthermore, Krafcik noted that any risks associated with the implementation of Lean could be reduced by better training, flexibility in the workforce, easy-to-build product designs, high-quality products, and an efficient network of suppliers.

Lean Thinking soon became popular in the manufacturing industry. Recently, Lean Thinking has been used in Software Development with great success. Furthermore, Lean has spread into several sectors, including healthcare, with an increasing number of companies starting to use Lean practices.

5.1 Lean Principles

Lean describes five principles that act as a framework to help businesses improve the efficiency and effectiveness of their processes. Lean helps managers identify inefficiencies in their process and steps in processes that do not offer any value to the customer. Lean Thinking encourages businesses to create better workflows where continuous improvement is made part of the culture. A company can be highly competitive, increase the value offered to clients, decrease production costs, and increase profits by practicing the five principles of Lean.

1. Define Customer Value

It is important to understand what value really is to understand the first principle of Lean Thinking. Value in Lean Thinking refers to the value of the product the customer is willing to pay for. Therefore, it's important to understand the exact requirements of the customer. Some features may add value to the product. However, the customer may not be willing to pay for those features for a variety of reasons.

The customer may not understand the value of those features. He or she may not have the budget. Irrespective of the reasoning behind a customer's unwillingness to pay for a feature that may add value to a product, it's important to understand what customers value and not—failing to do so results in high production costs and reduced profits.

For example, a camera can be developed with a feature that enables the user to upload a video to YouTube with a single press of a button. However, most customers may not be willing to pay extra for such a feature. Therefore, adding that feature to the product may not be profitable; nevertheless, it is surely useful and convenient.

2. Map the Value Stream

This principle focuses on identifying activities that contribute to values relating to the customer's definition of value. Any activity that does not contribute to offering value to the end customer is considered as waste. Such activities are broken down into two categories in Lean Thinking: non-value but necessary, and non-value and unnecessary.

A company should try to reduce the former as much as possible. However, non-value and unnecessary activities should be eliminated as they are pure waste. The reduction of the first category and elimination of the second usually leads to the development of a product that matches the value the customer is willing to pay.

3. Create Flow

The removal of activities that are considered waste and reducing activities that do not add value but are necessary can disrupt processes differently. Therefore, it is important to ensure a smooth flow of the remainder of the steps so that there are not any delays or interruptions in a process. Activities that can be used to create flow include the reconfiguration of the production steps, the breakdown of those steps, making the workload more even, the creation of cross-functional departments, and the training of multi-skilled and adaptive employees.

4. Establish Pull

One of the biggest wastes in any production system is inventory. This principle aims to limit inventory and items, and are WIP (work in progress) so that the current stock of materials and resources remain available for a smooth workflow. This principle encourages businesses to develop products at the time they are required, and in the exact quantities that are required.

Pull-based systems use the needs of customers to direct them. The customer's exact needs are determined, and the value stream is followed backward through the production system. It ensures that the products that are developed will satisfy the needs of customers instead of going to waste.

5. Pursue Perfection

The application of the first four principles reduces and eliminates waste. However, the fifth principle is considered the most important as it encourages businesses to chase perfection. Lean Thinking does not encourage businesses to relax once they achieve a smooth flow with minimal waste. Instead, it encourages companies to nurture a culture where teams continuously seek ways to improve. In such an environment, employees actively seek perfection with their activities. The company, its teams, and employees continue to learn with their processes, improving and evolving bit by bit every day.

5.2 Eight Wastes of Lean

Lean is a way of thinking focused on removing wastes from processes while adding value to products. Therefore, it is important to understand what is considered waste in Lean. Lean Thinking defines waste as any step in a process that does not add any value to the customer. Simply put, waste is a process that the customer doesn't find useful or is not willing to pay for.

1. Transport

Waste produced during transportation includes the movement of workers, tools and equipment, inventory, and products any further than necessary. Unnecessary movement can often lead to damages and defects of tools, materials, and products while putting workers at the risk of injury. It also results in unnecessary work, exhaustion, and costly wear and tear.

Waste in transportation can be reduced by placing workers who collaborate near each other. The materials and tools necessary for production must also be easily accessible by workers without unnecessarily moving around. Double or triple handling of materials should be eliminated. Many businesses use proper planning of production lines, using U-shaped production lines, enhancing the flow between processes, and avoiding the over-production of WIP (work in progress) items.

2. Inventory

Many businesses rarely think about excess inventory as waste. In a financial sense, bulk purchases allow businesses to be entitled to discounts, while inventory is considered as an asset in accounting. However, having more inventory than the necessary amount to maintain a steady flow of work usually leads to various problems, including damaged materials, product defects, increased lead times, unnecessary spending on inventory, and unidentified problems hidden in inventory.

Inventory waste can be many things depending on the business. In an office environment, it may be files that are waiting around to be worked on or records in an unused database. Broken machines, additional finished products, and extra materials occupying workspace are considered inventory waste in manufacturing. Inventory wastes can be reduced by only purchasing raw materials when needed, purchasing the required quantities, reducing buffers, and creating queues to eliminate overproduction.

3. Motion

Any movement of people, machinery, and equipment that is considered unnecessary is wasted motion. It includes unnecessary walking, reaching of all kinds, and physical movement to reach other workers, tools, and products. Tasks that may involve a lot of motion may be redesigned so that unnecessary motion is reduced as much as possible while paying close attention to health and safety standards.

In an office environment, the wasted motion includes activities such as reaching for materials like files, walking to a cupboard that stores files, unnecessary mouse clicks, and entering data twice. In manufacturing, activities such as reaching for materials and tools, walking to access materials and tools, and readjusting components after installation are examples for wasted motion.

Wasted motion can be reduced significantly by redesigning and organizing workstations, proper placement of equipment close to the workers who need them, and the placement of materials in ergonomic positions so that reaching for them is unnecessary.

4. Waiting

Any unnecessary waiting is considered waste. It includes workers waiting for raw materials and equipment, machinery and equipment that are idle, and workers waiting on other workers to finish work. Uneven production stations and flaws in processes often cause such wastes. In an office environment, waiting for waste may happen as workers wait for emails from coworkers, as workers wait for files to be reviewed, and the time wasted in ineffective and unnecessarily long meetings. Waiting for waste can be reduced by redesigning processes so that there is a continuous flow, making workloads more even by standardizing work instructions, and the development of multi-skilled workers who can quickly adjust to the demands of the work.

5. Overproduction

When a product or part of a product is developed before it is required, the result is overproduction waste. Businesses are often tempted to produce extra products so that they are available when required. They may see it as beneficial since workers and machinery are rarely left idle.

That type of production is caused by "Just in Case" thinking, which is the opposite of Lean Thinking. Overproduction results in increased storage costs, defects being unidentified due to the large amount of WIP—preventing smooth workflow—and increased lead-time.

In an office environment, making extra copies of files, the creation of reports that do not serve a purpose or interest others, providing unnecessary information and details, and doing a service available before the customer is ready are overproduction waste. Ensuring that the rate of manufacturing is even between stations—single-piece flow or manufacturing small batches—and the use of the Kanban Method to control WIP can usually reduce overproduction waste.

6. Overprocessing

Doing more work than necessary, adding unnecessary components to products, and adding features and steps in a product that are not required by the customer are considered as overprocessing waste. In manufacturing, the use of equipment that is unnecessarily expensive, using parts that have capacities beyond requirements, unnecessary analysis, and readjusting components after they have already been adjusted are some examples of overprocessing waste. In an office environment, the creation of reports that have too much detail, processes that involve too many steps, having unnecessary individuals sign certain documents, and having unnecessary forms are overprocessing waste examples.

Overprocessing waste can be reduced by looking at the work requirements from the customer's viewpoint. The customer should be in mind when designing and adjusting processes and workflows. Workers should also be encouraged to reflect on whether the customer would see value in each of their actions and if the customer is willing to pay for their work.

7. Defects

Products that are not fit for use are known as defects. Defects are usually reworked or scrapped. Reworking results in considerable waste since additional resources are required to bring a product to a usable state. Scrapping results in a total waste of time and resources spent on that product. Therefore, both results are wasteful as they do not deliver any value to the customer.

Defects can be countered by identifying common defects in a process and addressing those issues. Redesigning of processes so that they do no create products with abnormalities is one of the best ways to eliminate defects. However, there is always a likelihood of a defected product being developed; therefore, processes should be improved so that such products are identified before they reach the end customer.

8. Skills – The Eighth Waste

The eighth waste defined in Lean Thinking was not a part of the Toyota Production System. The eighth waste describes unused and misused human talent. This type of waste usually occurs when businesses separate the management of the processes from the actual workers. Managers are responsible for planning, controlling, organizing, and innovation. Meanwhile, employees are required to follow orders and do the work that managers plan and organize.

In such circumstances, the expertise and knowledge of frontline workers are wasted, and opportunities to improve processes are lost. People who actually do the work often have a better understanding of the processes in place and how they can be achieved. Therefore, they need to be encouraged to come up with solutions and ways to improve processes in a company instead of limiting them to "work."

In offices, poor incentives, insufficient training and coaching, ignoring employee feedback, and placing employees in roles below their qualifications, skills, and experience usually result in the wasting of skills. In manufacturing, skills are wasted when workers are not provided with adequate training to operate machinery and equipment, provided with unsuitable tools to carry out a certain job, and when workers aren't challenged enough to improve and come up with ideas to improve processes.

5.3 Lean Management

Lean Thinking is becoming increasingly popular among companies belonging to various sectors. As a result, there are many success stories where the implementation of Lean Thinking has helped companies reduce waste and increase profits while continuously improving their processes.

FedEx Express

This company is known throughout the world for delivering airmail and packages. The company maintains a sizable fleet of aircraft and ships that help transport cargo throughout the world. Aircraft maintenance is one of the main operations at FedEx Express that costs resources and space.

The global recession in 2008 forced FedEx Express to resort to Lean Thinking in a bid to save money during those difficult times. The focus on reducing waste and continuous improvements may have resulted in the decision to adopt Lean Thinking.

Before implementing Lean Management, the FedEx facility at the Los Angeles International Airport (LAX) managed to complete fourteen C-Checks per year. C-Checks are a type of aircraft maintenance checks. After implementing Lean principles, the maintenance crew at the same facility managed to complete thirty C-Checks per year. Prior to the adoption of Lean Thinking, it took the FedEx crew around 32,000 working hours to complete a single C-Check. However, the adoption of Lean Practices cut this time significantly, with the crew only needing an average of 21,000 working hours per C-Check.

One of the key reasons behind the drastic changes was the identification of milestones. The team identified 68 milestones that needed to be completed to complete a C-Check successfully. Doing so enabled them to make the workflow smoother while reducing waste considerably.

Nike

The athletic fashion label is one of the most popular businesses to benefit from the implementation of Lean Thinking. Nike has benefited by adopting Lean Management and continues to reach new levels of productivity and waste reduction year after year thanks to Lean Management.

The year 2012 was a special year for Nike as it released its first FY 10-11 Sustainable Business Performance Summary. It was the first Manufacturing Index released by the label. The FY 10-11 introduced several quality standards that would be practiced across Nike's numerous factories located all around the world.

These explicit policies and guidelines increased consistency between different factories while reducing miscommunications and misunderstandings common before the release of FY 10-11. Setting clear expectations brought consistency to Nike's processes across factories and increased the overall performance and quality of their processes. Furthermore, CO_2 emissions of factories declined by six percent during the time while production increased by twenty percent.

5.4 Lean and Agile

Both Agile and Lean are flexible methods focused on helping teams develop high-quality products sustainably while making gradual improvements. Both methods emphasize the importance of providing high-value products for customers delivered in short iterations instead of a single, long development cycle.

Agile and Lean share numerous values and principles. However, Agile and Lean are not the same; however, many individuals wrongly believe that they are. Therefore, some teams that practice Agile or Lean do not have a clear understanding of the similarities and differences between them.

Agile or Lean can be considered a good influence; however, they are most beneficial when implemented holistically. Failure to understand them often leads to unsuccessful implementations that do not bring the results that many companies hope to achieve.

Approach to Speed and Iteration

Agile teams aim to deliver usable software at regular intervals. Such releases often begin when the development is at an early stage. Early and regular releases enable teams to use valuable feedback from customers and adapt to change with ease.

Lean Management also has a similar principle where teams are encouraged to deliver fast. The faster a team can deliver value to their customer, the quicker they will get feedback from them. The difference between the Agile and Lean principles is that in Lean Thinking, teams increase the speed of delivery by limiting work-in-progress items. However, in Agile, teams rely on smaller development cycles to deliver working product increments quickly.

Customers First

Lean and Agile both encourage teams to focus on customer satisfaction as one of their primary goals. Agile teams ensure customer satisfaction by starting an early and continuous dialog with customers and facilitating changes that add value to products that are being developed. Customers are more involved in the development process and usually end up receiving a product that is full of value.

Lean teams focus on the customer by providing the customer with what they are willing to pay for. Lean Thinking considers anything that the customer is not willing to pay for as waste. Therefore, customers are likely to get exactly what they ask for instead of products with missing features or additional features that they do not find useful.

Role of Discipline

Agile recommends more structured teams and roles compared to Lean Management. Agile relies on defined roles, various estimation techniques, defined roles, systematic reviews, and many other project management practices. The disciplined nature of Agile processes allows teams to develop products faster and embrace change well.

Lean Thinking relies on discipline, but in a different way. Lean Thinking is successful when it becomes a part of a company's culture. Lean Thinking does not require teams to uphold external rules and expectations. It is more about every individual and team upholding Lean principles in unison.

Conclusion

Traditional project management methodologies that existed by the dawn of the twenty-first century were linear and sequential. These attributes resulted in projects running late, while teams struggled to deal with the later identified changes. The Agile Alliance that met in a ski resort in Utah in 2001 released the *Agile Manifesto* that described four values and twelve principles aimed at resolving issues that the software development industry faced at the time.

The values and principles of Agile focused on small, self-organizing, and cross-functional teams working on small increments of products that enabled customers to be more involved during a project's development phase. Customers would be provided with working product increments from an early stage in development. Each regular increment would give customers the chance to provide feedback and request changes.

The Agile philosophy recommends that teams embrace change instead of avoiding it. Change is inevitable in many projects due to failures in requirement gathering and analysis and quickly evolving market and customer needs. As a result, a methodology that can respond to change positively was welcomed by the software development industry. Agile soon became highly popular in IT firms while spreading to other industries, from healthcare and construction to marketing and sales.

While many companies realized the benefits that the Agile methodology offered, one of the main reasons for adopting Agile was the need for expertise and knowledge. Agile principles and values were difficult for teams to grasp, especially for those who had followed traditional project management approaches for years. As a result, the need for Agile frameworks with clear steps and guidelines emerged.

Scrum is an Agile framework that enabled organizations to become Agile without needing prior Agile experience and knowledge. Scrum provided clear guidelines on how to form teams, specific team roles and responsibilities, types of meetings or ceremonies that would help practice Agile values and principles, and several Scrum artifacts to guide documentation to lead teams toward project goals.

Kanban is a method that involved the visualization of workflows and processes with the use of Kanban Boards. The concept originated in the factories of the Japanese carmaker Toyota, while the Kanban Method was later introduced so that businesses across different industries could utilize it to improve team performance with the visualization of processes and workflows. The Kanban Method has many similarities to the Agile methodology, including striving for continuous improvements within teams and processes, among many.

Lean Thinking is another approach that has many similarities to the values and principles described in the Agile way of doing things. However, Lean Thinking and Agile are not the same methodology or approach. Lean Thinking focuses on achieving optimal productivity and product value by reducing and eliminating waste in processes. Lean identifies eight types of wastes along with five principles that guide teams to reduce and eliminate waste while continuously making gradual improvements to the way they work.

The Agile methodology has helped many teams achieve project goals through true collaboration. Its openness to change has made it one of the best methodologies for projects with varying requirements and evolving needs. Scrum is a framework that guides teams who are willing to adopt Agile values and principles. Similarly, Kanban and Lean are methods that can ensure the smooth flow of processes while eliminating waste and bottlenecks.

All these methodologies, frameworks, and approaches offer various advantages and disadvantages to businesses. Some of them may be more or less suitable for companies, teams, and projects. Therefore, it is important to clearly understand their values and practices, so the best methodology or framework can be chosen to manage a project.

Part 2: Scrum

What You Need to Know About This Agile Methodology for Project Management

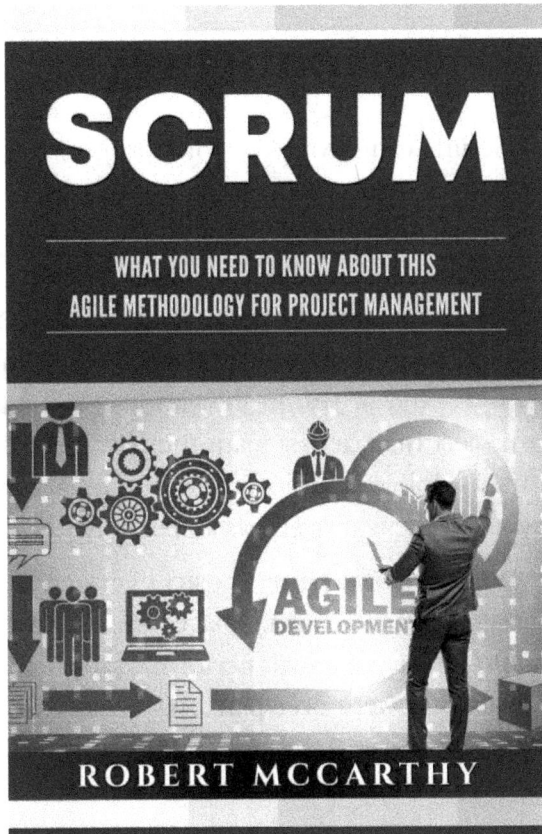

Introduction

Working with Scrum can skyrocket your project's success to new heights. Many project managers wonder if it's really possible to do more with less. You might have the same questions racing through your mind. Is it really possible to finish projects with fewer resources? Is it really possible to make projects more manageable, more efficient, and more fun, with a single project methodology? The answer: yes, yes and ... *yes*. In the various projects I embarked on as either a project manager or team member, one thing became evident: the methodology employed by an organization has an immediate impact on the team's efforts and results.

As a project manager or aspiring project manager, your success is your team's success; and vice versa. I have never seen a professional who didn't want to be part of a high-performing team and share in its wins. Professionals who were ever part of a highly-efficient and top-performing team can relate to this. In such teams, the collective energy is immense, leading to constant improvements in the products in development. Amazing results don't just "fall from the sky;" it's all cause and effect. And if cause and effect aren't adequately managed and channeled, they can delay or even block success

Without a doubt, a team that excels in cooperation, a team that flows, is one that achieves tremendous results with less effort. But a team on its own is not enough in the continuously developing world we live in. A team without the tools, techniques, and the framework to adequately deal with this dynamism, is like a ship without a rudder.

Fortunately, many visionaries, project managers, and entrepreneurs have woken up to the fact that the traditional way of working isn't suited for today's needs. Thus, they have developed new innovative ways to deal with projects from start to finish, called *agile methodologies*. Many leading companies, such as Microsoft, Apple, and Amazon, use an agile approach to tackle their projects adequately. These big tech companies are aware that continuous technological developments make such a flexible approach to handling projects necessary—maybe almost vital—to surviving. There are various agile methodologies present today, such as Scrum, Kanban, and XP. Scrum is the most popular method or framework, and this book will make clear how you can implement it in your organization or company for ample project success.

With Scrum, you are given a framework with which you can develop various products that are part of a project. The Scrum framework and methodology started out being used for IT-projects exclusively. Today, things are different. Scrum is used for every kind of project: from transportation to agriculture to engineering projects. Now, isn't that amazing? Thus, I'm adamant that learning about Scrum will be of much use to you and your team, no matter what field you are in.

The Scrum approach makes competitors using traditional methods look like snails, struggling day in, day out to move the project forward more swiftly. Taking on projects iteratively optimizes predictability of results, mitigates risks—or sometimes even eliminates them—and makes you and your team more efficient. This all falls in line with the three main pillars Scrum is based on, namely transparency, inspection, and adjustment/adaptation.

In this book, we delve deep into the most up-to-date manner of implementing Scrum. That may sound overwhelming, but don't worry. I'll simplify matters as much as possible and cover the essential aspects and processes of Scrum in an easy-to-understand fashion, even for complete beginners. And don't worry, this book also includes some more advanced aspects of Scrum for you more seasoned project managers.

With my experience managing different teams in several industries, I have faced many failures and setbacks in my work as a project manager. Truth be told, I'm not a "born" manager, not at all. But with hard work, consistency, and determination, I distinguished myself from most project managers. Doing so was impossible without the use of Scrum.

I want to help others do the same. Therefore, I aimed to write this book without the fluff, but with accurate and practical information. Information you can apply from the get-go to help you move forward as a project manager. Besides, the book will include various examples, expert advice, and real case studies to give a more precise image of the reality around Scrum.

In the first section of this book, we start by giving an in-depth explanation about how you can get started with Scrum. We explain what it is and why you need it. The second section outlines the Scrum process from start to finish. You'll learn about Scrum teams, breaking down a Scrum project, Scrum Artifacts, and much more! In the third section, I hand you the necessary Scrum tools, tips, and other essentials to skyrocket your projects' success. This is done by looking at Scrum metrics, how to excel in a specific Scrum role, common mistakes, and software tools you can use.

So, what are you waiting for? Read forth and set yourself apart from the crowd!

Chapter 1: Project Management: Past and Present

Every innovation has its history. The same goes for methodologies to manage projects. Nowadays, more organizations adopt what we call *agile methods* for project management. When you ask someone to describe the term *agile*, you're likely to get multiple different answers. Therefore, it is helpful to take a look at the origins of this agile-way of working. That's precisely what we'll do in this chapter. Furthermore, you will learn more about various agile concepts, its components, multiple benefits, and much more.

The Origins of Agile Methodologies

Before organizations practiced agile methodologies, they employed the so-called "waterfall method" to get through projects. Winston Royce first mentioned this waterfall method in his paper, *Managing the Development of Large Software Systems*, that he published in 1970. Royce proffered a diagram for software development, similar to the one you see below:

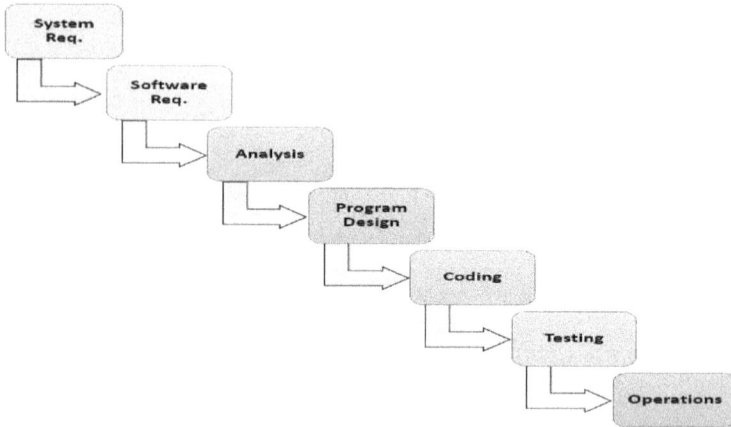

In the chart, you see the various phases of software development. Starting with the System Requirements and Software Requirements, it was possible to come to an analysis. Afterward, it was possible to design the program based on this analysis. When the design was ready, it was time to start coding and testing the software. Finally, the software would go to operations and would be used. As you see, each phase flows into a new one, without going back to a previous phase, similar to a waterfall. What I found particularly interesting to note is that Royce himself didn't see this method as optimal. This became evident in his paper when he described a more iterative and step-by-step approach of going through these phases (i.e., agile).

There is a reason the method goes through the phases like a waterfall. Remember that in the 1950s and 1960s, computers were as big as a house! They had various intricate parts that were hard to work with and needed professionals to change any of these parts. These computers were very time-consuming and complex to develop. Thus, the waterfall method was introduced to tackle this endeavor. There are numerous challenges involved by practicing this method. In the waterfall method, there are specialized people per phase. Just think of business analysts, architects, and designers, developers, QA specialists, and infrastructure specialists who did the deployment. The problem is the gaps between these activities and the need to transfer information between these phases. A lot of documentation was developed through each stage. The business analyst starts with the documentation and passes it to the designer who adds to it. Analysis and design together are what we call "Big Design Up Front" or, in short, BDUF. When the design is ready, the document is passed on to the developers. When they are done with the product, they hand it over to the testers. Afterward, they hand it over to the IT-staff who help the customers implement the software.

What usually happened was that when the developers were busying themselves with the program as described in the documentation, they found that what they had to create didn't work out. Then a change needed to be made. And this change was not found in the documentation made earlier. Now we have code that doesn't match the documentation—the same documentation that took the analysts and developers a lot of time to craft. Therefore, there had to be a way to go back to this documentation and improve upon it, remove parts, or add new elements.

Furthermore, within the waterfall method, *milestones* are generally used. These are detailed with a description and the date by which they should be achieved. However, in practice, it's challenging to always stay within the specified time frame. Sometimes more time is needed, making every defined milestone inaccurate. Also, the professionals in these phases didn't talk with the other professionals that weren't in direct relation to them. For instance, there is no clear communication between the testers and designers or analysts and the IT-staff.

It should be clear that this method is far from ideal in the rapidly changing digital era we live in today. Fortunately, there's a new, more agile approach to deal with projects. The new procedure was mainly created in response to the developments of computers in the 1980s and 1990s. Computers became easier to employ, and Software as a Service (SaaS) and the internet became available. In 1986, Hirotaka Takeuchi and Ikujiro Nonaka wrote a paper in the Harvard Business Review named *The New New Product Development Game*. In this paper, they delved into the phases of the waterfall method, namely: analysis, design, develop, test, and finally deploy. Besides giving more detail about the steps, they pointed out something very innovative. They showed that these phases don't only work on their own. In fact, the stages they proffered showed that the phases should have a very distinct overlap. Thus, information was better communicated between the professionals in each stage. For example, the analyst actively checks on the design and even looks at the development, from time to time. The paper suggests that the analysts should be around more frequently during the development phase, so that even at the end of the development phase, there is still a business representative (analyst) who can deliver the appropriate information.

Takeuchi and Nonaka described this process as being like a "scrum." This was derived from the Rugby term, when all players are linked together. Being linked together, they all work toward a common goal: trying to push the ball down the field. This symbolizes a team walking through the phases together, all the way to the end. Furthermore, from this paper, many processes, methods, and frameworks were developed and enhanced, such as Scrum by Jeff Sutherland and Ken Schwaber, Extreme Programming (XP) by Kent Beck, Kanban by Taiichi Ohno, and many more.

Fast forward to the 21st century, and current "thought leaders" have concluded that they're striving for similar goals. They are trying to achieve the same objectives to make processes more efficient, effective, and worthwhile. They found out that a lot of what they were doing in their methods has, in fact, a connection with other methods. The methods were more interconnected than the thought leaders imagined. Thus, because many of the core values in these methodologies were the same, they came together to bring to life what's called *The Agile Manifesto*, published in 2001. This manifesto introduced the world of project management to values it was in dire need of. It outlines that individuals and interactions are more important than processes and tools. But processes and tools still have a place; they just shouldn't intervene with, for instance, communication with stakeholders or professionals in a project. Besides, the manifesto values working software more than having comprehensive documentation. Don't get me wrong, documentation still has its place, but the actual, pure-practice of working with the software has the upper-hand. Customer collaboration is more significant than contract negotiation. Sometimes things change. Therefore, we must be able to have some form of dynamism in contracts; this isn't possible without adequate customer collaboration. In an agile approach, we value responding to change more than following a strict plan. No doubt, the adage, "If you fail to plan, you're planning to fail," sounds clear in our minds, but planning shouldn't be too rigid. Rigidness is what prevents organizations from moving through projects quickly. Moving quickly isn't possible without the flexibility to respond to changes swiftly.

Sometimes finding a more balanced approach between the values is necessary. In various organizations, people use tools such as Zoom or Skype for Business to make communication possible with remote workers or external stakeholders, using technology to support a focus on individuals and interactions. Therefore, extremes should be avoided. Each project should be evaluated individually to figure out how much each value should weigh.

The Key Agile Concepts

To develop a correct *agile mindset*, you should understand various agile concepts. The first concept you should know about within the agile-approach is **short feedback loops**. In the waterfall method, a customer may see no product for months, maybe *years* on end. If it turns out that the customer wanted a different feature or perhaps an entirely different product, it's too late. A key concept within agile is to get information to the customer as soon as possible, so they can find out ways to move forward in the shortest possible time. Thus, it's possible to fix things while the project is still running. The same goes for professionals, such as developers and testers, or even business analysts. With an agile mindset in place, every team member thinks "big" about the end product, but they work "small," so they can fall and get back up rapidly and learn from these missteps swiftly every single time.

The second concept is the so-called **just-in-time** way of gathering requirements and finishing the design. Frequently, developing software is compared to building a house. Honestly, it's nothing like building a house. There is no need to have complete blueprints outlining every intricate aspect of design from A to Z. What I've seen in practice is that development works exponentially better when working from a kind of "to-do list," as simple as that may sound.

The third crucial concept in agile is **delivering incremental value**. We cannot make a product entirely from the get-go. Thus, we make various parts of value along the way, working toward the end-product. Afterward, these incremental products can be discussed with customers or other stakeholders. Their feedback can be gathered, making room for improving this part of the end-product. The goal is to have incremental products that are ready to be released to the customer. This means, for software development, that it's integrated and documented thoroughly, the programmers have finished the code, and the program is tested and deployed.

The fourth concept is the **maintainable work rate**. You've probably experienced projects where things start easy, you work a little bit, and then find that a deadline is coming up soon, which makes employees work 80+ hour weeks all of a sudden. With agile, there is more control regarding the effort of employees. This effort should be equal during the entire project as much as physically possible. This way, employees don't get burned out, and they deliver better, more predictable results. Bottom line: you have to keep a pace that employees can maintain to get the best results for your projects.

Within agile, there is a concept of **Lean hierarchy and self-organizing teams**, and this is the fifth concept I'll address. This means that a few people make decisions instead of having an extremely slow hierarchy, where too many people have to say something before a decision is made. Doing it the *Lean* way means that it takes significantly less time when decisions roll out.

Regarding decisions for specific projects, self-organizing teams are essential. Therein is the central idea that the team is in the best position to make concrete decisions for continuing the project. Without self-organizing teams, there's usually a manager who makes these decisions while they aren't even aware of the intricate, crucial details within a project. Empowering self-organizing teams and allowing them to make decisions helps garner better results.

Values like **respect, collaboration, trust, courage, and transparency** are essential within agile methodologies. These give you the "agile mindset" to support the projects at work and are critical for **continuous delivery**, which is the sixth concept. When managers trust their self-organizing teams and there is a frequent enough dialogue, this makes projects very transparent. Delivering in short feedback loops makes continuous delivery a crucial concept. Any time the team builds something, it can take it from building and development to deployment as fast as possible. This comes in the form of continuous integration. For instance, as soon as I write some code, this is shared with other developers through a server.

We live in an age where most projects still "manage" change. In agile, we instead **embrace change**, then try to manage it. This is the seventh concept. Especially for customers, we always need to be willing to change things around in the product if it isn't satisfactory. Thus, changing becomes an integral part of the entire project, making it better to embrace change than manage it. Inspecting and adapting is necessary for any agile approach, be it Scrum, Kanban, or XP. This happens in the tools, but also the incremental products you deliver and even the team itself. These approaches are frameworks that demand your input. You have to fill them with what makes sense for you. Otherwise, embracing change will be a long, poor, tiresome road.

Scrum: How It All Started

Scrum was founded by Jeff Sutherland and Ken Schwaber approximately 25 years ago. After his military career, Jeff studied medicine at the University of Colorado. At university, he developed an interest in something utterly different than medicine: namely, IT. Schwaber, on the other hand, started his career early as a software engineer. Both gentlemen had a vision for a quicker, more reliable, and more effective method for creating software. They were frustrated with the inefficiencies present in the waterfall method and worked effortlessly to find a new way to tackle projects.

Sutherland, in his book *Scrum: The Art of Doing Twice the Work in Half the Time,* gives examples of these inefficiencies. For instance, take the digitalization project conducted by the FBI in 2006 for a new program called Sentinel. The program aimed to get rid of the paper processes to make room for digital operations. Any idea how much the project would cost? An immense $451 million. According to the contractors, the entire program, systems, and underlying processes would be up and running somewhere in 2009. Fast forward a few years later, from 2006 to 2010, and there was no working program, and the considerable sum of $451 million was already spent. In the following months, the stipulated project cost was far-exceeded, and expenses from the contractor didn't seem to stop. But there was no other option, because the project was already halfway, and it had to continue. Well, at least that's what they thought. Thinking this way is faulty. It's built on the premise that we should continue with a project no matter what happens because we've already invested a significant amount of time, money, and energy. This is called *the sunk cost fallacy.*

Long story short, the team hired by the FBI kept at it and estimated that the project should only take about six to eight more years. Oh yeah, and did I mention that an additional $350 million of taxpayers' money was needed? Although genius engineers, managers, and analysts were relentlessly working on the project, things didn't work out. Their process involved the same phases mentioned in the waterfall method. So, they would gather requirements, analyze these requirements, make a plan for the contractor, and add details with various features needed for the program. A group of very talented professionals from various fields worked for days, weeks, and months without stopping. After the plan was ready, they spent more days, weeks, and months planning the process for implementing the plan. To make this clear, they made sure all documentation was easily accessible, was nicely designed, and included various shining graphs and diagrams detailing the tasks and amount of work necessary.

The graphs and diagrams indicated what part of the plan should be implemented first before moving on to the next part. They included various stepping stones to get to the destination. After a couple of stepping stones, a milestone was highlighted. Between the tasks and stepping stones, the deliverables were made apparent. With the introduction of numerous software tools for creating graphs and diagrams, it was easy to keep adding more elements to them and making them more complex along the way. Eventually, you can't see the forest for the trees. Besides, these graphs and diagrams may look fancy, but they're nearly always wrong. Why? Because they aren't suited to a project environment that isn't dynamic. Developing software is a continuous and changing process. Doing so in a vacuum doesn't end up well, not at all, as we read from this example.

The managers for this project at the FBI thought they had all the resources to make the project a wild success. From great talent, as mentioned earlier, to advanced technology and software systems. But something was missing. Something that may seem subtle, but it's a subtlety that makes all the difference: people worked and planned wrongly, i.e., their methodology was invalid. Such a great and intensive project was never feasible with the old, traditional, inefficient way of working. There was a new, innovative, efficient way needed.

Fortunately, after a lot of blood, sweat, and tears, there was a time of joy. Finally, one of the genius managers realized that the plan made a couple of months ago was now a work of fiction, due to continuous changes along the way. When the manager took a closer look at the raw development process, and its similar products and services, they knew the plan was not at all valid. Eventually, they discovered that a new way to manage projects was vital. Thus, they were introduced to Scrum, one of the only methodologies to make these data-driven, complex projects a wild success. They realized that the way of managing projects in the past isn't applicable anymore. Going forth with this waterfall approach will cost a tremendous amount of resources.

Furthermore, the ideal outcomes are often not achieved. In the FBI example, the waterfall method of doing things cost hundreds of millions of dollars and a lot of resources. In the new, agile way of working, people can do more in less time. People can learn from mistakes and readjust in less time. And people can achieve better results in less time. Doing more with less is the motto within agile methodologies.

It may sound like a fantasy, but various organizations show amazing results with this approach. The agile-way works, and it works for all kinds of organizations. Sutherland and Schwaber found the method by looking at *how* people do their work, instead of listening to what they *say* they do. Both gentlemen studied ways to make projects more durable by looking at studies conducted around project management. Also, they took a closer look at how other organizations manage their projects. Doing so showed them a pattern of what works during projects and what doesn't. They knew there was something behind the successes of various businesses around the world.

They concluded that most successful organizations managed their projects in a more iterative manner, such as Amazon. Now, Amazon is well-known to implement Scrum not only in smaller projects but even in various business layers with larger projects. Do you want to learn how Scrum changes organizations for the better? Do you want to help your organization move forward quickly? Do you want excellent project success? Adopting a Scrum methodology will pave the way for excellent project outcomes. Let's have a more detailed look at what Scrum is about.

Chapter 2: Scrum: What It Is and Why You Need It

Now that we have a clear understanding of agile, its origins, concepts, values, and benefits, I hope it is evident why you need a more agile approach for project success. In this chapter, we'll delve deeper into the agile methodology—or framework—of Scrum. The difference between Scrum and other agile methods is that it's the easiest and most flexible method to implement. Contrary to what many project managers think, Scrum is not just for software development projects. As you read earlier, Scrum originated from the software development world, but it is nowadays adopted in nearly every reasonable-sized organization, regardless of the industry.

The Basics

Scrum doesn't require any advanced mathematics or rocket science. You could jot down the most basic Scrum elements on a Post-it Note. Take a look at the essential elements on which Scrum is based:

Plan the short term in detail, without forgetting the long term. Within Scrum, we know that detailed planning and schedules can only be used effectively in the short term. This is quite the opposite of traditional methodologies, where detailed scheduling takes place for events that are "light-years" in the future. This doesn't mean that a successful Scrum team doesn't think long term. Not at all. Team members think long term, but know that day-to-day scheduling of tasks in the short term will help them get closer to the long term objectives. Scheduling the long term in detail is far from possible because too many variables can change over time. It seems so logical, but many (project) managers seem to think the opposite.

Self-organizing and multi-disciplinary teams for the win. If you want to win big in business, you need a great team. Especially within Scrum, the team plays a central role and works more innovatively. It is a team that decides what it will work on, how long it will take, and when it is finished. No manager has any power to enforce their wishes on the team. The team consists of all the professional disciplines needed to get the job done. Team members know the work, and the manager usually doesn't. So, wouldn't it make more sense for these professionals to figure out what to work on and when things should be finished? A rhetorical question, of course. Team members within the Scrum framework craft the plan, organize the tasks, and carry out the work.

Chunking projects into reasonable sizes. Whenever you are faced with a large project, it's difficult to swallow the "elephant" in one bite. Instead, make reasonable-sized chunks to get it down the throat. "Chunking" or splitting significant tasks into smaller parts is crucial during any Scrum project. Within Scrum, projects are divided into short sprints, where you develop and deliver valuable incremental products for the customer.

Transparency is key. This is what Scrum is all about. With Scrum, no team member can "fool" another team member in terms of conducted work. This forces collaboration and helps the team members get the job done well and in a timely fashion. If you want to get things done and keep good relationships, there is only one way: communicate transparently. Only by communicating transparently can you achieve what you want in the best, fastest, and most enjoyable fashion.

The necessary feedback-loop. When you offer your customers the opportunity to give feedback, you know exactly what is going on with them and you can respond. In this way, customer feedback plays an essential role within your company. When customers and stakeholders regularly provide feedback on the product increment, this will hopefully bring about a better result.

Don't forget to communicate! The team regularly discusses with each other whether it can improve the working method, making it more and more effective. The intensive cooperation, self-organization, feedback, and fast results almost inevitably lead to more pleasure when doing the work.

As said, there are no advanced mathematics anywhere to be found. But still, millions of project managers manage ineffectively. People who hear about Scrum for the first time often say that they are already using all these essential elements. However, being able to "practice what you preach" appears to be the obstacle. The effectiveness of Scrum stands or falls with implementation. Experienced Scrum professionals know that it's not about whether you employ Scrum, but how well you use it. The outcome is the mark of the success or failure of the team's efforts, scheduling, and planning.

Scrum is still finding its place in different industries besides IT. Some industries have taken up Scrum very well, while others remain behind. In my experience, I have come across things that work slightly differently than in the traditional software industry. These points of attention are indispensable for the broad application and implementation of Scrum. To figure out if your organization is ready to use Scrum, answer the following questions, and count your points!

Are projects always done on time?

> Yes. (1 point)
>
> Once in a while. (2 points)
>
> Seldom. (3 points)

Do the projects never get mixed up?

> Yeah, that's right, I can always focus on a single project. (1 point)
>
> Nope, I have to divide my time and focus on various projects. However, I still have an overview. (2 points)
>
> No, it is all mixed up, and the work feels too fragmented. It almost seems like the organization is some "project carousel." (3 points)

Does your organization usually think and work in projects?

> Yes. (1 point)
>
> We are working on a more project-based approach. (2 points)
>
> We want to work on a project basis but are not yet geared to this. (3 points)

• **Would you say that other team members are motivated?**

> Yes. (1 point)
>
> Once in a while. (2 points)
>
> Rarely. (3 points)

• **Do the team members always deliver what the customers or stakeholders demand from them?**

Yes. (1 point)

Things often have to be redone; this costs a lot of extra energy. (2 points)

Stakeholders/customers are not always satisfied with what we deliver. (3 points)

• **Would you say that other team members exchange a lot of knowledge and skills?**

Yes, we learn a lot from each other and use each other's knowledge and skills. (1 point)

Once in a while. (2 points)

No, way too little. (3 points)

• **Does the team usually do the most important things first, and do the team members not allow each other to be distracted by side issues?**

Yes, we always tackle the most critical issues first. (1 point)

Once in a while. (2 points)

Many colleagues are busy with things that make me wonder if they are critical. (3 points)

• **Do you think that stakeholders are actively involved in the project?**

Yes, during the project, there are several moments when stakeholders give feedback and indicate their desires and wishes. (1 point)

Sometimes, because we analyze the stakeholders and invite them once in a while to check the progress. (2 points)

No, because I think that too many times, stakeholders are hardly involved in the process. (3 points)

- **Would you say that the team is flexible and can quickly adapt to changes in the desires and wishes of the customer or the project environment?**

> Yes, if anything would change, we can make adjustments in the short term without causing (m)any problems. (1 point)

> We can make adjustments, but that often requires a lot of art and work on-the-fly. Sometimes we even have to redo advanced projects. (2 points)

> We work according to a schedule that is difficult to adjust en route. (3 points)

- **Is your current working method providing much pleasure for the entire team?**

> Yes. (1 point)

> Once in a while. (2 points)

> Rarely. (3 points)

After you have answered the questions add up your score! The first answer option is worth one point, the second two points, and the third is—you guessed it ... three points. Now, let's see where your organization is currently at:

- If your score is 10-11: Your organization is already great at applying Scrum elements. Maybe the organization has several years of experience practicing Scrum or a different agile methodology. These skills can be sharpened by using more advanced techniques, described in a later chapter.

- If your score is 12-21: You're doing fine, but there is a lot of room for improvement. The organization is most likely implementing various Scrum techniques and elements, but they don't go too well yet. This guidebook will help you improve on the probable pitfalls.

- If your score is 21-30: Your organization needs to change. A considerable change needs to happen to save your organization's project because working in the same ineffective and inefficient way will be detrimental to the organization and the people involved. This book will set you up to implement Scrum to a very good degree. Thus, your organization can change things around for the better.

What Is Scrum?

Scrum is an agile methodology to tackle projects. It is based on a fundamentally different vision of working together so that many traditional project pitfalls are avoided. Most people have experienced or heard about large project teams that, after months of work, deliver half-finished products that no one is waiting for. With Scrum, we do the exact opposite. We cut the large project into pieces and finish small parts every few weeks. This is done in sprints: relatively short periods of two-to-four weeks, during which we realize and deliver parts of the project. Customers can see a more rapid and better result, and can give immediate feedback. This allows us to respond much better to customer requirements.

Scrum is more than just a vision. It's a practical method to work productively with a dedicated team. The core of Scrum is explicit and consists of roles, ceremonies, and lists. There are clear roles so that everyone knows where she/he stands, fixed ceremonies in which the team comes together, and a few handy lists that replace extensive, highly-inefficient plans. It is essential to have a good understanding of this and use the Scrum elements in the right way: only if you do so correctly is it possible to say you're working with Scrum.

Scrum consists of three roles, four ceremonies, and four lists. Scrum has three distinctive roles. You form a Scrum team with people who together can do the most substantial portion of the tasks at hand. The group consists of an average of seven people, plus or minus two, often from different disciplines. The team is self-organizing. This means that the team members decide together how they want to carry out the tasks and divide the work. A Scrum team has *no* project manager. You might think, "No project manager? Then how do the team members know what needs to be completed and when?"

Well, first of all, the Scrum team has people from all three roles, namely the Scrum Master role, Product Owner role, and Development Team role. The latter is different than the phrase "the Scrum team" because it doesn't include the Scrum Master and Product Owner roles. Instead, it contains professionals from various disciplines, such as business analysts, designers, and programmers, to take care of the tasks. Furthermore, the Product Owner is the delegated principal for the project, i.e., the one who gives the project to the Development Team and has close contact with the customer(s). She or he makes an inventory of the wishes of the internal or external customer(s) and translates this into a clear assignment for the team. The Product Owner monitors the job, the priorities, and the preconditions and makes decisions where necessary. The Product Owner "owns" the product or the content. And then there is the Scrum Master, the facilitator of the Scrum team. The Scrum Master guides the team so that the process runs smoothly. The Scrum Master is therefore responsible for the quality of the process: ensuring that the Development Team takes the right steps and that ceremonies take place in the right way and at the right time.

Scrum ceremonies occur as four different types of team meetings. The lead time of the project is divided into equally significant periods called sprints. Every new sprint starts with a sprint planning meeting, in which the team determines how it can achieve the most important goals for this sprint. During the sprint, stand-ups (i.e., daily "Scrums" or stand-up meetings) are regularly held. These are short interim discussions of no more than fifteen minutes, during which the team members tell each other the progress of the tasks. Standing keeps the team members going and prevents people from leaning back and losing interest. At the end of every sprint, the team presents everything that was made in this sprint to the Product Owner. This is called the sprint review. Sometimes other stakeholders are also invited, such as colleagues, customers, or directors. The fourth type of ceremony is a final retrospective meeting. In this meeting, you and the team look back on the process, so that you can improve team performance in the next sprint.

When I started with Scrum in my previous job, we did ask a Scrum coach to guide the teams during the first sprints. The basis of Scrum is simple, but applying it well in practice is a craft where coaching is more than useful. The Scrum coach then immediately trained several enthusiastic colleagues and me to become a Scrum Master.

Now, we arrive at the last indispensable part of Scrum, the lists. The four Scrum lists are nothing more than visual aids. In Scrum, you usually display the lists on flip charts with Post-it Notes, that show what the team is working on. The first list is the *Product Backlog*, the overview with all requirements and wishes for the entire project. With Scrum, you no longer have to write an extensive long-term plan, but the Product Owner makes an inventory of the components that must be worked out for this project. For each part, a separate Post-it is placed on the Product Backlog, and these are called the "backlog items."

At the start of every sprint, the Development Team selects, along with the Product Owner, the items from the Product Backlog that the team will realize in the coming sprint. These Post-its move to the second list: the Sprint Backlog. On the third list, a "definition of done" is then written for each item. These are the requirements that a thing must fulfill to be considered "done." The "definition of done" answers the question: What exactly will be finished and achieved at the end of the sprint, and what does that look like? Formulating this with the team creates a shared image of what you will deliver at the end of this sprint. Also, there's an extension to this list that's usually ignored: "the definition of fun." This is a list of conditions for making and keeping work within the Scrum process fun. An essential element of preparation for the team is the Scrum board, which the items of the Sprint Backlog are placed on. The purest form consists of the columns "to do," "busy," and "done." The Scrum board can be digital but is usually made on a physical whiteboard or flip chart.

Is Scrum Needed?

There are many reasons why Scrum is needed when you work on various projects. Below I'll give multiple reasons why you need to use Scrum for your projects as soon as possible. However, please take notice: I could name many more reasons to use Scrum for projects. And many other reasons are scattered throughout this book. For this chapter, the reasons below will suffice.

The first reason is that you gain more value from your resources, such as time and money, but also talent. With Scrum, it is always clear what team members are working on, and product increments are delivered as fast as possible. The most important parts of the end-product are usable early on because of this. Therefore the "Time-to-Market" of a product can be drastically shortened.

The second reason is that Scrum gives the team more control over the whole product creation process: from beginning to end. Scrum is an empirical process, and by forcing yourself to get feedback as quickly as possible, a lot of information is garnered. This information also gets better and better, and stakeholders can employ this information to help move the project forward. This contrasts with traditional methods, in which setbacks usually appear when the project is "nearly finished." Most of the time, it's then too late.

Furthermore, the third reason is delivering higher quality products for customers and/or other stakeholders. By asking customers and other stakeholders for their opinion during every sprint review, you never lose sight of the users' wishes and desires. This gives you an edge over other organizations that don't have this continuous process of checking and validating projects in place. The Scrum approach helps to get a better understanding of what is really bothering customers. In the process, everyone learns what's important. By doing production-based product increment deliveries every time, the attention to detail and quality is great. This is far superior to making a ton of assumptions in the beginning, and then facing the problems further down the line.

Another good reason to use Scrum is that it allows you to explore uncertain, more complex projects without losing too many resources. Instead of having long and expensive documentation done by several external consultants, it can be gratifying to put a Scrum team to work on several sprints. After a few weeks, you'll know whether a new product is feasible. If not, better luck next time, at least you learned something. If it works out, which happens often, then you're immediately ahead!

Besides, Scrum results in less bureaucracy. In line with the previous point, many organizations have become much more cautious about spending resources like money and time due to bad experiences in the past. Thus, procedures have been developed to avoid these. After a while, these procedures have taken on a life of their own. Therefore, frequently, these procedures take a long time. Mainly because work is waiting for approval from Change Advisory Boards and the like. With Scrum, these obstacles disappear.

As you can see, the basics and reasons for applying Scrum are straightforward. No advanced math to be seen. However, appearances are deceptive. Behind the simple roles, ceremonies, and lists, is a fundamentally different way of working. The combination of these factors makes it work. Always remember that a too dogmatic approach to implementing the concepts is far from ideal; for yourself, for your team, but also for the organization. Therefore, you must not blindly apply all of the Scrum elements we discuss in this book, without realizing the value for your specific project. Instead, you should evaluate your project and your team's needs and cater your application of Scrum to those needs. Besides the essential Scrum elements described earlier, there are many more elements you can use during a Scrum project, as you'll see in the coming chapters. Add to the basics by selecting other concepts and elements that you're pretty sure will get your team moving the most. Don't be afraid to add a new perspective to elements where you think and feel it's necessary. Without further ado, let's delve deeper into Scrum!

Chapter 3: Scrum Roles and Responsibilities

By employing the waterfall method, it isn't until the last phase that your customers get to interact with the product. Then is the time you get to know if what you produced is what they were looking for. Because it is right at the end of the project, what can be done if the customer isn't satisfied? If a few requirements are outdated? Or, if a couple of elements are missing? This is an absolute recipe for disaster because people don't know what they want, until they interact with it!

Scrum is great for getting the ball rolling quickly in projects. Scrum functions as a framework for self-organizing teams to conduct projects effectively and efficiently. It consists of three categories you must know about, namely: roles, artifacts, and events. During the explanation of these categories, I will add additional insights for properly implementing them. These insights may or may not be based on The Scrum Guide by Jeff Sutherland and Ken Schwaber, but they seem essential to me when dealing with Scrum processes. This chapter is dedicated to the roles in Scrum.

Product Owner

In Scrum, there are a couple of roles. The first role is the Product Owner. The Product Owner strives to maximize product value; that is their responsibility. Whatever we do in a project should create, deliver, and keep value for the customers and organization. The Product Owner makes sure this is the case.

Furthermore, she/he manages the Product Backlog, which is the only document or source where all the requirements are listed. It is the Product Owner's job to make sure the Product Backlog is well-formed, makes sense, and is prioritized. Also, the Product Owner represents the customers by often communicating with them. Finally, they make so-called go/no-go decisions, for what will be released and what will not. Finding the right person to fulfill this role is difficult, because of the wide variety of skills necessary to complete these tasks correctly.

The Product Owner takes ownership of the product and is responsible for its successful realization: on time, within the stipulated budget, and with satisfied customers. All three have to be met for a successful project. Missing one of these three aspects means missing delivering a great product.

Scrum preaches simplicity and transparency, and the role of the Product Owner is an excellent example of this. After all, there is only one Product Owner, and that is the same person during the entire project. This way, everyone knows who makes the decisions. Decisions about the direction of the product, that is.

Moreover, every Product Owner only has one product under her/his care, and that is all she/he focuses on. This gives a clear image to the Product Owner and results in a more significant commitment. Why? Because the Product Owner will spend all their time on directing the product until it is finished. Typically, the Product Owner will spend half of the time with the stakeholders and the other half with the team. The role of the Product Owner is a full-time job.

Although various skeptics might disagree, the Product Owner needs to be full-time, because the work that needs to be done is extensive. The Product Owner is not only concerned with the team, and perhaps more things are being developed than just software. The Product Owner is involved with stakeholders for a considerable part of the time. This includes all kinds of activities, such as discussing with customers; coordinating with the marketing department; making sketches to get a better picture of the target audience; and coordinating the budget with the management.

It is important to note that the Product Owner shouldn't cause a bottleneck. This will result in unnecessary costs because the professionals have to wait to get to work. So, the Product Owner must have enough time to be present, to show the way, to motivate people, and to repeat the vision.

It is the responsibility of the Product Owner to represent anyone with an interest in the product and to weigh the interests between all these people or parties, and to constantly decide what is essential. Indeed, I say "constantly" because, as everyone knows, the demands and wishes of these stakeholders are continually changing.

The Product Owner is also responsible for discussing with the Development Team about the implementation of the requirements and wishes of the stakeholders. The Development Team usually has several ways to interpret and implement a requirement. The costs can, therefore, vary considerably, and the Product Owner must understand that decisions are made by the Development Team as well. In the discussions with the Development Team, it is mainly about the "how" and the "what" in terms of cost.

With these two aspects of requirements: "what" and "how," the Product Owner prioritizes the needs or items listed on the Product Backlog. She/he weighs up the order in which the objects are realized. This is often done by presenting the estimates of the

Development Team to the stakeholders, so that "quick wins" are put forward. Besides, it is possible that some requirements may even be canceled due to costs, for instance. When you are the Product Owner, prioritize first, then ask for costs. Cost estimates take a relatively long time, so pay more attention to the most vital issues. It is your primary responsibility to get value for money. You want to get a return on your investment (ROI) of time, energy, and money.

There is always the possibility that things won't go as planned. Thus, you could also mess things up. Just take it on the chin, these things can happen. The development of new products remains an uncertain and complex undertaking. After all, that's why we use Scrum. Scrum is not the guaranteed pathway to success. However, it is a guaranteed way to uncover all challenges, opportunities, and possibilities, as quickly as possible. Many successful companies use Scrum to get started and test the business case, even though the chance of failure is significant. If it works out well, they know they have won time, money, and other resources. If things flop, because the team will not be ready on time or there aren't enough funds, for example, then they know when to stop much earlier than in traditional methodologies. Therefore, even failing with Scrum is better than with any other way! Because you lose the least amount of resources, get back up quickly, and start working on the next thing in line without hesitation.

As explained earlier, the main task of the Product Owner is managing the Product Backlog. As a Product Owner, you are always (re)prioritizing the items on the Product Backlog, so that the most valuable things are placed at the top. These are the items with the highest value and relatively lowest costs. The Product Owner must always prioritize all requirements and wishes on the Product Backlog based on business value. These items should get an estimate of the effort required by the Development Team. This is called "backlog refinement," also known as "backlog grooming." The Product Backlog is very dynamic, mainly because the Development Team often demonstrates valuable, production-ready software, and stakeholders gain new insights as time progresses. However, variables like budget, market needs, and the actual use of product increments that are developed each sprint, have an influence too.

The Product Owner needs to have a knack for making the Product Backlog as valuable and understandable as possible. The Product Backlog is primarily a communication tool and can benefit a myriad of people in the organization. Furthermore, it can be the source of many questions and discussions, but there is nothing wrong with that. It is better to ask questions straight away, rather than letting these roam around in people's heads. This would never be possible if the Product Backlog is in someone's drawer collecting dust: that's not the way to go. Instead, hang it on the wall or designate a whiteboard for it, to make it visible to anyone who has pending questions.

Also, nobody understands a Product Backlog full of jargon. Usually, if that is the case, it will lead to numerous issues, like poor acceptance by users, poor communication, and far less value for time, energy, and money. There are already enough organizations with a far too complex infrastructure. So, don't make things even more complicated, or it will bring forth many disadvantages. Instead, only list recognizable and usable points for users on the list, written in the words of a user. Go to production as quickly as possible and as often as possible (yes, go live!). Nothing gives more insight into the correctness of your decisions than the use of the product or product increment by real people.

Scrum Master

The next role is that of Scrum Master, which can, to a certain degree, be compared to project managers from traditional methodologies. So, just imagine yourself in this role. A Scrum Master is like a shepherd of Scrum because they need to know the concepts and implement the right mechanisms. They make sure everyone adheres to the agile values. As a Scrum Master, you should serve the

Development Team, but don't tell them how and when they should do their tasks specifically. Also, if the team has problems that get in the way of producing excellent results, you should remove any barriers by identifying the issues and removing the obstacles.

Finally, as a Scrum Master, you also focus on resolving conflicts so that the team is back on track as soon as possible. The main difference between project managers is that you, as a Scrum Master, are there to empower the team. You aren't there to be in command and tell every team member what they should do. You should leave them to do their work because they're specialized in that work. A team leader can take on the role of Scrum Master, but this is usually the case when a team is more mature. When the organization is new to working with Scrum, it's difficult for you as a team leader to juggle between being a Scrum Master and leading a team. You may get too busy educating people on the process so that there is no room for other activities. Therefore, it may be advised to have a specific Scrum Master per team. When the teams mature more and you gain more experience as a Scrum Master, you can be the Scrum Master for multiple teams. How come? Because with practice the teams will become more self-aware, self-resilient, and self-actualizing. Thus, you will have less work as a Scrum Master in terms of educating the teams and putting out fires, so to speak.

One of the most significant responsibilities of the Scrum Master is that she/he makes sure the team members adhere to the "rules" of Scrum. A Scrum Master ensures that the Scrum process runs optimally. Therein, we find the most significant difference with the Product Owner, who makes sure a great product is delivered. Without a doubt, all roles in Scrum work toward a common goal, but they have various responsibilities. A Scrum project has one Product Owner, one Scrum Master, and one Development Team, all of which ensure that the common goal is achieved. What is the common goal? Well, it's to realize the Product Owner's vision, i.e., realizing the product and doing so as efficiently and effectively as possible.

You, as a Scrum Master, should make sure that the rules of Scrum are followed. During the process of completing tasks, impediments or obstacles will naturally come forth. Then you, as a Scrum Master, should step up to remove those barriers. Besides, the Scrum Master must convince people that working according to Scrum leads to better results. Thus, you can connect with more stakeholders and team members, making the process of production more manageable. To make things clear, everything that you should do as a Scrum Master stems from these responsibilities:

- Removing impediments or obstacles the Development Team faces.

- Making sure everyone adheres to the rules of the "game." Guarding game rules.

- Get people on board with Scrum, organize support for Scrum.

- Create positive change in the organization utilizing Scrum properly.

You, as a Scrum Master, are similar to a referee and coach. You are a referee because it's your responsibility that every team member adheres to the Scrum rules. You are a coach because you facilitate the entire process for all team members. You remove obstacles and help move the team forward toward project success.

As a Scrum Master, it is, therefore, vital to organize everyone's support for Scrum. Make it clear that Scrum is not the goal but the means to achieving the team's goal. Scrum is a very suitable approach to realize a product that is complex.

The person you should first have a discussion with and get on board is the Product Owner, no questions asked. If you don't have her/him on board, the process will be like climbing a huge mountain. When the Product Owner is ready to go, both of you can start motivating the team to follow Scrum by explaining why it would lead to better outcomes. As a Scrum Master, ensure that you don't take over the responsibilities of the Product Owner. The Product Owner motivates with regard to the product. And the Scrum Master motivates team members concerning the process of creating the product *using* Scrum. You don't wait to start the Scrum project until "everything" is ready and perfect. Scrum emphasizes the process of continuous learning, especially learning by doing. If you don't take proper action as the Scrum Master, the project will stagnate.

There are phases every Scrum team goes through when starting. In the beginning phase, everyone is busying themselves learning about Scrum, and the corresponding rules. After the rules are understood, you can only really *know* them by pure practice, i.e., doing a project using Scrum. After the team is more mature, in the second phase, it can add more advanced tactics or strategies to perform the projects more efficiently and effectively. Finally, the last phase is mastery, where the team performs projects according to Scrum, almost effortlessly. The aim should be to get to the second phase as soon as possible. There is no other way than consistently clearing projects with Scrum. Achieving mastery at anything might take years and years of hard work. The same is the case for the last phase. Thus, it is no problem to stay in the second phase for a more extended period.

Whatever you do, know that Scrum is a powerful concept, used by thousands of organizations worldwide. Don't think too swiftly that you know it all and can make your own version of Scrum. It is imperative that you garner support from management and that they understand that the investment in Scrum is a long-term investment. Make it evident that you, as a Scrum Master, can't fix everything alone and may need help from other professionals. Besides, the management and other stakeholders should know that Scrum is also a tool for meaningful discussion, to gain commitment from everyone. Obtaining commitment is done best with education. Give a workshop regarding Scrum or a presentation where you outline the benefits and case studies. Besides, you can regularly talk about the process. This last point is, of course, possible in the sprint retrospective, a Scrum meeting I'll soon address, but you could also have a chat when you feel some stakeholders show some degree of resistance to Scrum or changes in general.

Making sure that everyone adheres to the rules is far from easy, especially if your team is new to working with Scrum. People have habits to take care of their work, and these are difficult to unlearn. Scrum encourages cooperation and transparency, everything is visible, and nobody in the team has ownership of parts. So, it often happens that team members have difficulty with their new position in the team, and it is your responsibility to bring that to their attention and make it discussable. To further illustrate this, let's say we have two testers in the Development Team, and they have the ingrained habit of making a test plan based on a functional design. They are used to the developer delivering the software at the end of a release, and they test the software for a couple of weeks based on their plan. However, in Scrum, things are different. Because in Scrum, we no longer make a functional design in advance, and a tester will have to contribute something meaningful before the software is ready. What does a tester do in the first days of the first iteration? And what about the business analyst? These are all questions the Scrum Master needs to tackle. This is a role with many challenges, in which you can use all your experience, but especially all your persuasiveness and communication skills. Fortunately, you are not alone; after all, you share a common goal with the Product Owner, Development Team, and many stakeholders.

Scrum makes it possible to readjust quickly when things don't work out. If the Product Owner missed some requirements on the Product Backlog, or stakeholders don't want to collaborate, then that will result in much more pain when using Scrum than other methods. As a Scrum Master, you may be inclined to ease the pain and even pick up some work the Development Team is struggling with. However, don't do this, but instead, show and ensure visibility of the problems and only remove obstacles that are blocking the Development Team from doing the work. Don't do the work itself, but pave the way for the work to be done!

The rules of Scrum help you as a Scrum Master to bring issues to the surface. The daily stand-up meeting, for example, and the sprint review at the end of each sprint, give you every opportunity to get people to have their say. This information is essential to you as a Scrum Master. It allows you to find improvements. For instance, when there are problems in the realization of a feature that jeopardizes the planning, bring them up, and ask the team to discuss alternatives with the Product Owner. When a team member mentions a specific problem for many days, make sure there are some small tasks on the Sprint Backlog to tackle these issues; we will cover this in more detail later.

I've mentioned something about "rules" numerous times, but what are these "rules?" The most important ones are listed below, but don't worry if some concepts are still unknown. These will be addressed later. The rules are:

> • In Scrum, there is one Product Owner. The Product Owner is responsible for the success of the product and has the mandate to make decisions regarding the product.

> • There is one Scrum Master. She/he ensures that the Scrum rules and principles are adhered to, so that everyone can optimally concentrate on their task to make the product or product increment.

> • In Scrum, there is one Development Team that independently develops the product. They do the tasks to get it in production.

- Scrum is done in sprints. These are continuous iterations of two to four weeks. Shorter is better. Sprints start and end on set days.

- All requirements and wishes for the product are recorded on the Product Backlog, which is managed by the Product Owner. The Product Backlog is always prioritized by value for the business, and the feasibility and cost of items on the Product Backlog are estimated by the Development Team because they know and do the work.

- A sprint starts with a sprint planning part 1 meeting, in which it is determined what will be dealt with in each sprint. Generally, these are the items at the top of the Product Backlog.

- Subsequently, in sprint planning part 2, the team—in the presence of the Product Owner—determines how the work is done and how they will progress the work.

- Every sprint, a number of tasks are moved from the Product Backlog to the Sprint Backlog. By doing this, these more significant Product Backlog tasks are split into smaller tasks the team can tackle on a daily basis.

- Also, making progress transparent is necessary for the Development Team as well. This is done through a "burndown chart."

- The Product Owner and the Development Team have made agreements. For instance, it's clear what is meant by a finished Product Backlog item. This is written down in the definition of done. "Done" means: so good that it can be taken into production.

- Every day the team holds a Daily Scrum meeting or stand-up meeting for not more than fifteen minutes. During this meeting, the Development Team goes through the tasks of the Sprint Backlog together, utilizing several standard questions. This meeting is public, and stakeholders can listen. They can only observe and must not interject during this meeting.

- At the end of the sprint, there is a meeting named "sprint review." Therein, the Development Team shows the results to the Product Owner and internal/external stakeholders and then receives feedback. The team only delivers the results that are "done," i.e., that can be taken into production by users.

- After the sprint review is completed, the team holds a sprint retrospective to pause and discuss how things went during the sprint. What went well? What can be improved? Make sure agreements are made, to enhance the process of the coming sprints.

Development Team

The third role within Scrum, as you might have noticed, is the Development Team. Within Scrum, everyone is developing something, so everyone is a developer (not necessarily a software developer!). All the professionals are part of the Development Team, be they an HR professional, software engineer, or business analyst. When you are on the team, these professional labels fade away, making you more aware and focused on the team's goal and working together. These teams are cross-functional or multi-disciplinary. So, they consist of the professionals necessary to come up with the product increments. That is what makes them self-organizing teams; the team knows design, programming/developing, testing, and any more skill sets needed to carry out the project successfully.

They should decide what they will work on and how they will do it—without much, or any, external help. In a Development Team, collaboration is crucial. So, if there is a problem with testing or more effort is needed in that area, a business analyst in the product team can jump in and lend a hand. Being collaborative means that you may give up some of your responsibilities or take on some extra tasks to accomplish the objective. Finally, the team shouldn't be too large.

The Development Team does all the work to turn a Product Owner's vision into a working product. They do all the direct work to complete the product. No one works directly on the product before or after the team starts or is finished. This means that the team gathers the requirements, performs analysis, makes a design, takes care of the underlying architecture, implements the product (increment), does the testing, installation, and documentation. This is all done by a multidisciplinary team of around five-to-nine people. Could Scrum work with more people? Well, not in the same team, as that leads to too much overhead. Adding people to a team is already less effective at eight or nine because you'll lose focus and commitment. What about using Scrum with fewer than five people? This could be possible, but then the Scrum Master or the Product Owner usually has a double role. That is far from ideal. You can't use Scrum with one or two people. What would one person do during the stand-up meeting? Of course, it is possible for one or two people to incorporate various Scrum elements into their processes, but not Scrum in its entirety, because Scrum is a team sport!

For example, if you are developing a communication system with the programming language Python, you may need an assisting architect, two Python developers, a business analyst, and a tester. If the communication system requires a fresh design or some form of interaction, then you add a CSS expert to the team. Various projects could consist of a wide variety of professionals. Even though the Development Team in Scrum is multidisciplinary, this doesn't mean that all experts within the team need to have interdisciplinary skill sets, such as: a professional who can program and do design work too. Indeed, team members sometimes do tasks that aren't in their appropriate skill sets. For instance, if the tester is very busy, a developer might jump in and take some of the tester's tasks. This makes it evident that Scrum is all about making the team win! Just think about it in a sport like a soccer/football when Team A is behind 1-0. Team A gets a corner kick, and it is the last minute of the game—then even the goalkeeper will come forward. The goalkeeper is aware that it isn't the natural position of a goalkeeper, but it is all for the higher purpose of winning.

Furthermore, the Development Team is responsible for ensuring that all work is done. The team should be mature enough to get going after the Product Owner discusses the requirements. Of course, it is sometimes possible that some specialized knowledge isn't present in the team. The team could then search for external help or expertise. These activities remain the responsibility of the team. Don't forget that the team is self-organizing. Another important aspect within Scrum is that we work with fixed teams, which work together sprint after sprint. Therefore, the team grows together, and the team members become more attuned to each other. A good Product Owner needs to know how much time the Product Backlog items—such as requirements—cost. Thus, the Product Owner needs estimates. And who is better to deliver these estimates than the Development Team who have the experience and have to do the work? Do not make the classic mistake of making estimates as a Product Owner or Scrum Master, or leaving it to one of the people in the team. The entire team gives the estimates. I still find it unreal that in some organizations, a manager makes these estimates while she/he has no understanding of the work at all. Fortunately, in Scrum, things are different. By adequately executing Scrum, you gain much more insight into the progress and control of costs. The only thing is that you have to start.

Scrum is a process that is intended for work that has a more complex nature, like product development. These are uncertain ventures, with a clear purpose, but without a clear trajectory to traverse. Due to the dynamism of such projects, planning anything in detail upfront is ridiculous. There are too many variables we can't predict before actually doing the work. This makes in-depth planning unnecessary, to say the least. Many dynamic projects fail, because estimating the tasks is done poorly. Scrum is an empirical process in which we are in a constant "learning mode." Everything we learn is used in the coming sprints and put into practice straight away. Thus, things like designs, programming code, and documentation are always being tailored to the desires and wishes of the customers or end-users.

Once all the work has been planned during the sprint reviews, the Development Team can get started. The team makes the Sprint Backlog by hanging the Product Backlog items and related tasks on the wall or a whiteboard, forming a so-called "Scrum board" by making the sections "To Do," "Doing," or "Done." This gives everyone a good overview of the work in the current sprint, not only for the team but everyone who enters the room and takes a look at the Scrum board. Besides, the progress is tracked by the team in the burndown chart drawn out on another whiteboard or flip chart, and placed next to a note with the team's "definition of done." Thus, the ideal line of progress and how much of the work has been done is indicated, including when we can say the product (increment) is finished.

To further illustrate this, take the following example. Let's say the Development Team works together from Monday through Thursday. Every day starts with a stand-up meeting. This is a quick team consultation first thing when the team members arrive. It is advisable to do it first in the morning, for example, 9 a.m., or 9.30 a.m. if that suits the team better. This is much better than mindlessly checking pending or new emails. Instead, this daily stand-up meeting intends to coordinate work for the coming day. The earlier in the day, the better. It keeps the team members focused so that they can get to work straight away without wasting time. Remember that this is the moment to synchronize and not to report. There are other meetings to report on progress. It is a meeting of the team, just like construction workers on a project have a work meeting in the morning. They would discuss things like, "Oh, this morning, it's likely going to rain, so I'll take care of fixing the roof first, before other tasks." A colleague could say: "Well if you're fixing the roof anyway, I can take care of my task regarding the antenna simultaneously. I'll go with you."

This example falls in line with many of the Scrum values or principles, namely: Dedication, Focus, Openness, Respect, and Courage. These are important to deliver the best possible product; better than the Product Owner might have envisioned. You can always "hack" the system by giving high estimates to things that the Product Owner cannot estimate or verify. How to deal with this will be addressed later, but always realize that you are developing a product for the Product Owner. Try to support it with all your expertise, discipline, focus, creativity, and a sense of responsibility. And if you do not believe in the product, then it is your job to give your say respectfully; be open about it! The Product Owner will only benefit from this in the short—and long—term because this openness or transparency tends to result in better products and more customer satisfaction.

After a week or two, ideally, it's time for a critical moment, namely: the sprint review, wherein the Development Team shows the finished work to the Product Owner and stakeholders. The entire team works toward this moment, to give a demo and receive feedback. The team should always embrace a mindset of growth. When this is the case, the team would rather hear that something is good or not, because this gives them time to readjust and grow in the process to deliver even better products. During the demo, the team can show more than just the screens/webpages or the system. Think about things like test results and documentation. This is useful especially when stakeholders from the management team are present. Instead of a demo, the Development Team can also ask stakeholders to take a seat behind the team's development machines to try the system. Due to this hands-on approach, the stakeholders can get more of a feeling of the system and hopefully give better feedback. Let each team member guide a stakeholder, and make notes of the questions, comments, and especially the feedback. This way, you kill two birds with one stone, by immediately designing a part of the user acceptance test.

After the stakeholders have provided feedback, the Development Team withdraws to reflect on the final period. The sprint retrospective meeting allows the team to take the time to improve. Scrum encourages teams to evaluate the processes and performance of tasks because that is the way to keep growing. It is essential that a team takes the time to review what could be improved and to take a serious look at what is not going well. There are, therefore, no outsiders present at the sprint retrospective. The Scrum Master and Product Owner can join this meeting because both are part of the Scrum team that works toward the common objective.

However, it is vital that all team members feel at ease to share their experiences, missteps, and wins. There are many techniques to craft a retrospective meeting, and this will be addressed later on. For now, you should know that during this meeting, the team members figure out a few points for improvement. Think of things like: "Keeping the stand-up meeting to only fifteen minutes," "Asking an external consultant for advice," or "Making better adjustments to the 'definition of done.'" There is always something that could be better. Especially when the team is new to the world of Scrum, plenty of things go wrong, and that is just logical when starting.

It is the Development Team's responsibility to agree on a couple of concrete actions to improve working with Scrum at the end of the sprint retrospective meeting. Also, committing to take care of these points is necessary—take the following points as food for thought:

- Start the daily stand-up meeting at 9 a.m. and not later.

- Work more in pairs whenever possible.

- Jot down when a team member is absent in a shared file.

- Make more time for the Product Owner to refine the Product Backlog.

In any project, having the right team with the right competencies is essential. But where do we look when we gather our All-Star team? If you are responsible for assembling the Scrum team, you need to know more about how to do this adequately, because the team can make or break any project. So, are you ready to gather your All-Star Scrum team for project success? Let's do this!

Chapter 4: Scrum Teams: Gathering Your All-Star Team

Prioritizing your backlog and working on the items is not a task that is done in solitude. With various stakeholders, the essential things are selected to work on. Before any work takes place, you have to form your "All-Star" Scrum team. The Scrum team is not just a team; it's a multidisciplinary team. Depending on the project, the team should include people with various expertise, such as designers, developers, and business analysts. Every team member is aware of the collaborative nature Scrum is based on. Therefore, no one minds lending a hand and sharing responsibilities for the greater good of achieving the sprint goal. I've learned from experienced Scrum practitioners that they would prefer a "decent" designer, for instance, who fits well in the Scrum team and surrounding culture, than an "outstanding" designer who doesn't. When recruiting someone for the team: make sure they follow the rules; don't mind lending a hand (even if it's for something they are not directly responsible for); and that they fit in the culture.

When you are the one responsible for gathering the team, you should have a few qualities in place. Having these qualities in place is the difference between forming a simply "good" team and a "magnificent" team. These are a few top qualities:

Integrity. Too many people talk about integrity and its importance but don't know what it actually entails. What do we mean when we ensure integrity in a project, or when we work with integrity? The exact definition depends on the context. The context we address here is having integrity in a project environment where Scrum is employed. With this context in mind, the definition mentioned by Cambridge Dictionary fits nicely: "The quality of being honest and having strong moral principles that you refuse to change." Every Scrum Master has to deal with some problems on the team. Having a strong sense of honesty will benefit yourself, but also your teammates. When no one in the Scrum team trusts each other, when people aren't honest, outcomes will be far from desired. The same goes for following the Scrum principles and rules. As a Scrum Master, you should be first and foremost in adhering to these rules and an exemplar in terms of integrity too.

Show responsibility. When you show responsibility as a Scrum Master, it is easier for the team members to show responsibility for their tasks as well. As a Scrum Master, you have to plan any of the reviews, stand-up meetings, or other ceremonies. If you lack in this area, it will snowball to the Development Team and eventually to the product that the team aims to deliver. I'm a fan of the definition shared by The Nottingham Trent University, which states: "Responsible leadership is about making sustainable business decisions that take into account the interests of all stakeholders, including shareholders, employees, clients, suppliers, the community, the environment, and future generations." I like this particular definition because it makes clear that responsibility is more than self-responsibility. Of course, we need to be responsible for our tasks and finish them with great effort, but there is more to it; responsibility doesn't stop there. By applying Scrum, you will develop a greater sense of responsibility for the product to be delivered, due to the emphasis on collaboration.

Be friendly. I don't know of anyone who would want a manager or Scrum Master who is rude and continuously complains to every person on the team. Instead of being frustrated all the time, be the friendly one. Be the one who brings people up when they are down. Be the one who listens to others and tackles problems as soon as they arise. Be the one who makes the difference between a good and a great team. Behaving positively and being flat-out friendly can change your team's performance for the better, even if the team is filled with beginner Scrum practitioners.

To get more into the process and practicalities: usually, the Scrum team consists of around five-to-nine members. All roles should be represented: Product Owner, Scrum Master, and Development Team. The team should have professionals for all the needed skills to undertake the project. There is not a "one-size-fits-all" way of organizing your team. This depends mainly on the type of project and organization, but there are a few common ways to organize a team.

  o **Focus on customers and end-users.** A product being developed during a Scrum project may have a number of variables and numerous types of users. Having an organization based on customers facilitates the development process, because it makes the team focus on what the customer actually wants and not what the team *thinks* the customer wants.

  o **Focus on products.** These types of teams are usually seen at start-ups because they don't have the amount of complexity larger companies have. Thus, products can be developed with less-complex features at a faster pace.

o **Focus on features.** When working on a project, the team wants to focus on adding, removing, or innovating features. This is especially useful if the product to be developed is too significant for a single team to move forward.

o **Focus on a combination of factors.** Though there are various ways to organize your team, it may well be advisable for your team to take the best of these mentioned **ways** of organizing. Thus, a combination of focusing on the customer, products, and features, are most useful in practice. Otherwise, the team might focus too much on a particular subset, while the project is interconnected between multiple subgroups, such as the different customers, products or types of products they desire, and specific features for each type.

Besides the sprint planning, we should take a look at how the Development Team members work together. Within Scrum, we work with multidisciplinary teams with various expertise. Let's say we have two user experience (UX) designers, three software developers, and one tester. The UX designers focus on the look of the product increment; they make various mockups, wireframes, and more. The software developers write the code for the product increment, and the testers make sure test cases are taken care of. As you may consider, this can still create various boundaries, as we've seen in traditional methodologies. These boundaries may be physical but also organizational. What if the designers want to keep on designing until everything is "perfect?" And what if the developers want to write all code "perfectly" before they discuss it with the tester? Because they're not finished with the tasks, they sit in separate rooms. This is far from ideal. Therefore, make sure you take care of the following to avoid the pitfalls of traditional methodologies:

○ **Make sure the professionals sit together.** You all are a team for a reason. A team is meant to be close to each other and not in separate rooms. Let the team members sit with the professionals they work with in the sprint. Place their desks next to each other and remove the physical boundaries as far as you are capable.

○ **Don't wait.** Please, make sure not a single team member is waiting at all. Instead, *embrace the iterative-way of working* proclaimed in agile methodologies. For instance, for the designers, show early sketches to the developers. And developers, when you are done with the first half page of the product increment, show it to the tester and explain the details. Afterward, the testers can figure out a proper way of testing the product increment, interacting with the developers for clarity. For example, testers could think about: "What happens if the customer adds an 'and' in the search function?" More of this will be discussed later, because these types of waste are crucial in Scrum projects.

○ **Limit "work in progress."** Like the previous point, this isn't necessarily something within Scrum but more from Lean and Kanban. Despite this, it can be a factor that changes the overall outcomes of your Scrum project. Thus, make sure you limit "work in progress" concerning the various team members. For instance, if the software developers pound through and finish three pages, but the tester can only test one page, this creates a bottleneck in the process and leaves the tester overwhelmed. With a team that embraces iterative and collaborative working, this is easier than you might think. Work on one thing, e.g., one page, finish it, and go to the next thing.

When the Scrum team works, it is essential to have a continuous flow day in, day out. UX designers and software developers are designing and developing the software. The developers are writing a unit test and testing what they are doing, to a certain degree. Then, this work is checked into a source control that is hooked up to continuous integration. Continuous integration helps the team to design quality software faster. Also, it helps deliver new functionality to the customers or stakeholders more quickly while the developers become more productive and improve the quality of the software. With the continuous integration tools such as the ones created by Google Cloud, you can create automated builds, perform tests, deliver environments, and scan artifacts for security vulnerabilities, all in a matter of minutes. Continuous integration is essential for making your team work like "one body." In short, here are a few benefits:

- **More efficient development and improved productivity.** Accelerate developer feedback by running builds and tests on machines that are linked via high-performance networks. Perform builds in parallel on multiple computers for rapid feedback. This results in spending less time detecting errors.

- **Scale to the moon without worrying about maintenance.** Are you worried about the lengthy design and test times your team faces when it grows? There are various tools for continuous integration that scale automatically. This allows the team to make a hundred or maybe even thousands of builds when the amount of team members or projects grows.

- **Make secure incremental products part of your team's efforts.** Don't figure out security at the end of a sprint. Make sure security is checked continuously. If the team members don't want to take care of this on their own, make sure you get some tools in place to do that. Many tools can scan for security issues as soon as new artifacts are introduced. They even give the option to export detailed reports on the impact of these security issues and possible solutions. Besides, it's possible to set policies for different working environments.

Thus, only verified artifacts would have a place in the end-product.

• **Grant your team more flexibility.** With continuous integration software, you can pack your source code in Docker containers, for instance, or non-container artifacts. This makes it possible to build tools that we see in many organizations, be they small or large, such as Maven or Go.

When a new code is checked into this system of continuous integration, it immediately picks it up and builds it with everything else. This should be understood in a team that frequently works in the same code base, such as Go. When this is the case, the second a developer checks something into the source control; she/he knows if it makes anything break that someone else developed. Afterward, you can focus on running feature testing, such as the search feature. Usually, in preliminary stages, the testing will be manually done by team members.

For customer satisfaction, testing is imperative. It is crucial for our customers that the product the team develops works well. That means that there are no errors, bugs, and that the product does what it should do based on the set requirements. In Scrum, the developers test whether what they have developed works, but for large projects, this is a lot more complex and time-consuming. A simple search feature form will, in some instances, quickly have dozens of different outcomes, or scenarios, based on the form. All these scenarios must be checked. Fortunately, we can automatically test these types of scenarios using various tools or software. Although automating testing is great, it is not always possible. A disadvantage of automating this process is that setting up automatic tests takes time and money. Clear agreements with the team must be made about which scenarios are and are not being tested, how often they are tested, and what a test looks like. Tests must then be written and looked at by various experts working on the product. Many types of tests can be automated, but with a user test, this is a bit more complicated. Manual testing by the target group is usually essential here.

On the other hand, there is tooling to measure user experience automatically. Automatic testing can provide a sense of false safety. Nevertheless, it is essential to monitor the tests and the product increment the team is working on. It could be a feature of a website, application, or webshop. Thus, automating tests doesn't mean that no team member has to do anything to get this up and running. However, when everything is up and running, it will have a tremendous effect on the team's productivity in the long term.

What you have to remember is that testing is not something done at the end of the sprint! Testing should be done (nearly) every single day the team gets together. Continuously testing makes possible bottlenecks visible and allows the team to adjust rapidly, whenever necessary. This is the concept of inspecting and adapting at a micro level, namely within a sprint.

At first, if the team members are new to Scrum, they might see working in these small increments as less efficient. Such as when a developer says, "I can develop more pages, why do I have to wait?" Well, the developer may be able to develop ten things, but we can test only three. Developing more is not useful, because we cannot release untested code. Later down the line, this approach of sometimes doing less will be worthwhile, because nothing—or very little—has to change to make things work at the end of the sprint. Letting every professional take care of her/his work in its entirety before discussing was a critical element in how projects were tackled in the past. However, this resulted in many frustrations, because a lot had to change further down the line. With Scrum, these changes can be taken care of immediately after the professionals have discussed their progress. Therefore, in a later stage, there's not much to "clean up" or repair, which saves precious time and money.

Chapter 5: Scrum Artifacts

Besides particular roles, Scrum has multiple artifacts. In practice, we see that Scrum teams start with a so-called "product vision." Even though this is not necessarily part of the Scrum Guide, I've noticed that projects struggle without one. Without this artifact, it is difficult—maybe even impossible–to move forward in a project and garner excellent results. The product vision helps us get on course concerning dealing with the project. It makes clear who our target market is, who are the people who will need what we produce during the project, and what their desires are. What challenges are they facing? Also, the product vision should be clear about the specific business need or opportunity the team is going after.

Furthermore, it describes the key elements that are necessary for the product that will be developed during the project. Lastly, there should be a thorough understanding of what value the project will deliver to the organization. Usually, the "why" is vague for people working on the project, making it difficult to work hard toward the goal. The "why" could be anything from the amount of money made for the company to creating more impact for your specified market.

Another critical artifact that may not be part of the Scrum Guide is the release plan. Although it is not necessarily part of the Scrum Guide itself, in any project we have to know the game plan, and the release plan eases this process. Answers to questions like: "How are we going to tackle challenges and overcome unknown obstacles?" and "When will things be delivered?" are forecast entirely based on empirical data. Empirical data is data on how the team has performed in the past. So, it's not about how we think we are going to do it, but what the team members have proven that they *can* do. You should know that the release plan has an overlay on top of the Product Backlog. It tells us how many things of the Product Backlog we can get done in every short feedback loop. Also, the release plan is updated every sprint because while we work, we gather more and more empirical data on how the work is going, and if the team is on the right track. Below you'll read more about the most crucial Scrum artifacts found in the Scrum Guide.

Product Backlog

Probably the most crucial Scrum artifact is the Product Backlog. This is one of the two primary lists used in Scrum. This is the artifact that is managed by the Product Owner, as explained earlier. Why is this artifact so key? It is vital because it's the source of all the things that are required in the incremental product. It is a well-ordered and well-prioritized list of all functions, requirements, fixes, and enhancements for the incremental product. There is no other artifact or document where requirements are listed. All team members refer to this artifact, and this one only; there shouldn't be multiple versions going around.

The Product Backlog is the list that contains everything that needs to be done to create the product. It is that simple, and things shouldn't be complicated for no reason. The idea is that you know what to do, and that everyone knows what has been agreed upon, but that the work still has to be done. Scrum is not just starting without a goal or direction; as the product vision shows. But, in Scrum, we recognize the fact that things change during the work process and we constantly evolve as a team. That is why the Product Backlog is never a static list of items. New insights mean that new things will be added to the Product Backlog; earlier issues will be removed if they have been tackled; and the order of the items can change around. The development of new products is too complicated to realize with a preconceived plan. The Product Backlog is far from being a preconceived plan, it makes room for the innovative and dynamic projects we face nowadays. The critical point is that the Product Backlog only answers the "what," i.e., the properties of the product in a functional sense. For example, the function "Add to cart." The goal of the Product Backlog is not to explain the "how," for instance, how the Development Team should go about figuring out the "Add to cart" backlog item. That is the team's job to figure out.

By limiting yourself to answering the "what," everyone involved stays on board. This backlog is made for everyone: the team, but also internal and external stakeholders. Thus, it is imperative to make it understandable for every party involved, be they technical or non-technical. Although the "how" is not answered in the Product Backlog, it is good to have an explanation of "why" a particular item is listed on it. When the backlog is clear and free of jargon, it makes for a very efficient communication tool and entices stakeholders to engage in meaningful discussions.

The Product Backlog is managed by the Product Owner. The Product Owner is the boss of the Product Backlog. Only the Product Owner can determine whether something takes place on the backlog and with what priority. As a team member, never use your possible technological know-how, or whatever know-how you may have, to get things on the Product Backlog. In other words: as a Product Owner, don't include items on the backlog that come from the team that you don't understand. If they explain it and it becomes clear, you can always add it to the backlog. However, if you are in doubt, do not add it to the backlog. Usually, you can identify these questionable items, when a team member uses words such as "generic," "regret," and "later," in her/his explanation.

I hope you've figured out by now that the items on the Product Backlog are called Product Backlog items. Yup, not very innovative, but it does the job. What we usually see in real Scrum projects is that these Product Backlog items are formulated in user stories. User stories are a particular way of describing functional requirements on the Product Backlog. These stories aim to specifically express the functional wishes of users. This will be explained later on. However, not everything on the backlog is a user story or requirement. Various types of items can be part of the Product Backlog, such as:

o **Problems.** During the project, multiple bugs or issues can appear that need to be fixed to move forward. So, don't create any other spreadsheet or document with bugs or the like. These should have a place on the backlog.

o **Requirements.** Of course, requirements have a place on the backlog too. These can be of numerous kinds, such as functional requirements, non-functional requirements, system requirements, et cetera.

o **Desires and wishes.** When working on the product, stakeholders can deliver feedback and share their insights. The same is true for customers, and they can desire certain features. If the team sees the value in these matters, they can be added to the Product Backlog.

When these types of items have a place on the backlog, this creates more transparency. After the backlog items are defined, it is time to prioritize them. The essential backlog items need to have a place at the top, and they need to be in order. To facilitate this process, you can make use of the MoSCoW method, which is a method to prioritize tasks and come to a common understanding with the team members, (which job should be dealt with first, which one after that, et cetera.) MoSCoW is an acronym for the following:

o **Must-haves.** These are the requirements that have to be in the end-product. Without these, the product is useless.

o **Should have.** When the "must-haves" are taken care of, these should be tackled next. These are the matters that are very desirable, but the product could survive without them.

o **Could have.** These are requirements the team should only embark on when there is time remaining in a sprint.

o **Won't have.** These are the matters that won't be taken on in the current sprint(s) but may be useful in future projects.

Using this technique is useful, but make sure the team doesn't fall into some common pitfalls. What can happen is that team members will put all—or too many—items in the "Must have" category. Always double or triple check if these things are vital to bring the product to life. Furthermore, team members can be biased when the items are categorized together. Thus, you could let everyone categorize the items themselves first and then discuss each team member's categorization. This leaves room for discussion and brings about valuable insights. As a team, we should dare to come up with simple solutions that leave space for adding complexity in later stages of production. Figuring out simple solutions can help to deal with tackling the backlog items, because larger projects can have around 55-65 items. In practice, you could even come across an organization with hundreds of backlog items. In short, this is far from ideal, and more than likely the Product Backlog is far from optimized. Always reassess if the backlog can be improved upon and readjusted. If the backlog seems to contain too many tasks, see if it is possible to combine similar jobs or reduce the number of tasks if they aren't necessary at the moment. Doing so will keep the backlog clean and clear. Even this type of clustering can be done in silence by the team members to avoid possible biases.

	A	B	C	D
1	**Priority**	**Estimate**	**Description**	**Remark**
2	200	8	As a vacation shopper I want to compare different types of transport so that I can	
3	400	2	As a vacation shopper I want to receive a summary of my booking in my e-mail.	Make sure a summary appears on the webpage after booking and an email gets sent instantly afterwards.
4	1200	4	As an administrator I want to generate and track affiliate links	

Example initial Product Backlog

Furthermore, you should note that more than 85 percent are functional requirements. If you spot a lot of technical requirements or bugs on the backlog, this should alarm you that there are some serious issues with the quality of the product. If you're not sure if a backlog item should be removed, a cool technique to help you get more clarity is called "five times why." This technique enables you to figure out the root cause or underlying problem of the backlog item by asking "why" five times. Thus, you can evaluate if it makes sense to leave it on the backlog or not. Below is an example of the method.

Let's say there is a backlog item concerning a customer who is receiving orders late three times in a row.

Why Number 1: Why did the customer receive these orders too late?

Answer: The transport company, responsible for the delivery, did not have the correct address details of the customer.

Why Number 2: Why does the transport company not have the correct customer address details?

Answer: The address on the shipment does not match the address of the customer.

Why Number 3: Why does the shipping address not match the customer's address?

o Answer: The customer moved to a new location three months ago, and this new address is not yet included in the supplier's customer database.

Why Number 4: Why is the customer's new address not yet included in the supplier's customer database?

o Answer: The administrator forgot about it and has been ill now for a couple of weeks.

Why Number 5: Why didn't anyone think about changing the address?

o Answer: No one besides the administrator has the right to make a change to the customer database.

Furthermore, there is a technique for sorting the Product Backlog items by having stakeholders vote on the items regarding their importance. For instance, this can be done by giving everyone two to three votes and having them distribute these over the clustered backlog items by placing a dot next to them. If the votes are divided and the order becomes apparent, as Product Owner try and get rid of as many items as possible with the lowest or no votes. Just think about it: if there are forty votes to be distributed among twenty clusters of backlog items, then you can safely throw away every item with two or fewer votes. You can use the same technique with stakeholders to elicit more responses.

Seriously, the power of just eliminating stuff is far underestimated. Nothing is easier than not implementing items: it takes no time, has no bugs, no maintenance, and no documentation! Pay attention to the stakeholders' emotions. Some items with few votes can be essential for a stakeholder, so if you're thinking of throwing an item away, before you do have a good discussion. It is strange that someone finds an item very important, but that nobody else seems to care. Perhaps there is no support, and the stakeholder must accept that. Probably there is no understanding, and the stakeholder must create support. As a Product Owner, you can encourage your stakeholders to give their say about the decision they made. If this brings up issues you can't solve, then you know some issues need further investigation. This makes you aware of probable obstacles right off the bat, which is much better than learning about these problems when it's too late in the process. To illustrate this further, it may be that a particular stakeholder is much more important than the average stakeholder. Give them more opportunities to have a say so that it is clear to other stakeholders their opinion has a significant impact. In the coming chapters, you'll learn more about the practicalities of the Product Backlog, such as making proper estimates and crafting user stories. However, for this chapter, we'll take a look at a few more critical artifacts.

Sprint Backlog

The second crucial Scrum artifact is the so-called Sprint Backlog. This artifact is derived from the Product Backlog and can be seen as a plan for delivering the backlog items for each short feedback loop. The Sprint Backlog contains all the items for the sprint the team is currently working on. In the Sprint Backlog, we find all the tasks to fulfill a backlog item. For example, take the backlog item: "Banner Area" for a web design agency building an e-commerce website. The user story for this item is: "As a marketing professional, I want to be able to make an advertisement so that I can get customers for our products." Corresponding tasks that will appear on the Sprint Backlog are: "Make a banner area on the website," "Give the marketing professional the right to place a banner on the website," "Test if the banner is available for customers."

Furthermore, the Sprint Backlog is an artifact owned by the Development Team and not by you as a Scrum Master or Product

Owner. The team comes up with it, and they manage it and keep it up to date. Of course, the Sprint Backlog is dynamic and should be made readily available and visible.

At the start of the sprint, the Sprint Backlog is created during sprint planning. The most logical thing is to take the top items on the Product Backlog and use these as the basis for the Sprint Backlog. But it may be useful to choose a slightly different composition depending on the goal you want to achieve during the sprint. This is determined in the first part of the sprint planning meeting. It may be that the Product Owner links a number of items together that form a theme, so that the Development Team can take the product into production at the end of the sprint. It may also be that based on the latest sprint review, other choices are made, rather than simply picking up the items at the top of the Product Backlog.

The velocity of the team determines the number of items that are picked up; that is the number of points (story points) that a team can tackle in a sprint, and this is typically based on the results achieved in the last sprint (more on this later). It may, of course, be that a team member is absent or that someone is on training. Then it is good to adjust the velocity somewhat.

When filling the Sprint Backlog, be realistic and do not take on more tasks than you think you can handle. Especially after a disappointing sprint, inexperienced teams sometimes want to gain some confidence by taking up fewer items. Choose as much work as you can deliver based on recent results. In the second part of the sprint planning, the team will go through the items in more detail and break them up into more technical parts, so that it becomes clearer what exactly needs to be done. This is the time when the items on the Product Backlog, which mainly describes the "what" and "why", are translated into tasks that describe the "how." These more detailed tasks, together with the original Product Backlog items, make the Sprint Backlog.

The Sprint Backlog is created by—and for—the Development Team, as a tool to make the division of work clear and to monitor progress during the sprint. To be more transparent, the team generally shares the Sprint Backlog with everyone. The best way to do this is to hang the Sprint Backlog on the wall of the team room or to write it on a whiteboard to create a "Scrum board" (this is a board with the Product Backlog items you take on in a specific sprint and the tasks extracted from each item). Use markers, paper, and Post-it Notes to create a Sprint Backlog: it's that easy. You can use colors for various types of items, for example: green for Product Backlog items, red for bugs, et cetera. You can also give tasks-in-progress a label with the name of the people who are working on them. Make the board your own, but don't forget to add the fundamental Scrum elements first.

It is up to the team to determine the level of detail that it needs to complete the tasks. When the team has discussed the Product Backlog items and the Sprint Backlog is ready, the work can begin. However, always make sure the Development Team has made a substantial commitment to the Product Owner.

Burndown Chart, Impediment List, and the Definition of Done

Two other important Scrum artifacts are the burndown chart and impediment list, which track the work that remains each day. The burndown chart provides a visual of how many hours are remaining to deliver the incremental product of the sprint. If you are updating the Sprint Backlog, there isn't much difficulty in updating the burndown chart for the Development Team as well. The burndown chart is purely to get a quick view of how the team is performing and to see if it is on track timewise. The burndown chart can be displayed on a whiteboard or digitally with a flat-screen. The essence is that, like the Sprint Backlog, it is readily available and visible. No team member should be able to overlook it.

The next Scrum artifact is the necessary to be visible impediment list. For this list, we jot down anything and everything that could block or affect the route and slow down achieving the objective. The Scrum team should update this. If you are the Scrum Master monitoring the team's progress, this artifact is crucial. You could add to it, but the Development Team should do this first and foremost. If something can't be fixed at the moment, this can be escalated to the Scrum Master, who will find other professionals to take a look. However, this doesn't mean the Scrum Master owns it.

In every sprint, it is essential to have a "definition of done" for the team. In previous chapters, we've spoken about the definition of done. It is not exactly a list, but it is related to the lists. It answers the question: What do we mean when we consider that the work is "finished?" Agreements have to be made beforehand to decide what finished should be. This can vary wildly from project to project, but the standard is that "ready" in Scrum means that you can take it to production. The definition of done is crafted by the Product Owner and Development Team. For instance, let's say a fictional software company called xSoft Solutions wants to make a "definition of done." The Scrum team should consider these components:

- All the code is written and meets the agreed standards.

- The work has been functionally tested. Does everything work as it should for end-users?

- There is documentation available when needed to explain certain parts or features.

- Et cetera.

The definition of done can be jotted down on a piece of paper and placed next to the Sprint Backlog or Scrum board.

Chapter 6: Scrum Ceremonies, Meetings and Agendas

Within Scrum, there are various events or ceremonies. Most people don't find difficulties in attaining knowledge about Scrum, but do so when implementing the knowledge they garnered. This chapter demystifies the execution process of Scrum, by looking at the sprint planning meeting, working as a team, holding the stand-up meeting, quality control, and how to groom your Product Backlog.

First, as previously discussed, we start things off with the sprint planning. Selecting the items to work on should be done with the knowledge of past performance and capacity. If team A, for example, has been consistent in delivering four backlog items each sprint, this can be taken into account. The same goes for capacity. If, for example, a team member becomes sick, this void should be taken into account. Make clear *how* the items will be delivered in the Sprint Backlog: all the tasks you need to do, such as documentation, testing, design—whatever it is to finish the product increment.

The Sprint Planning Meeting: Execution

The complete Scrum team will be present for the sprint planning meeting: The Product Owner, Development Team, and Scrum

Master. Besides factoring in the team's speed when executing backlog items, team capacity should not be overlooked. Will all team members be present during the sprint? Is a team member going on vacation? Will the whole team visit a seminar? Et cetera. A backlog item at the top may be switched with another less intensive backlog item that fits well with the available capacity. No matter what the capacity, having a reasonable pace to tackle the backlog items is vital. The team should only bring in the items they feel they are most likely to complete entirely.

Furthermore, you should determine your sprint length. The length varies on the project and availability of team members. You shouldn't go shorter than one week and not more than four weeks. Once you have determined the length, stick to it. Bring more items in if the sprint was finished earlier. With the length in place, identify and jot down a sprint goal. This goal has the character of a mini product vision. It will give a general idea of what product increment the Development Team is working on.

To further illustrate this, take the fictional e-commerce company: Pineapples Inc., which is working on a new website. When the Pineapples Inc. team held the sprint planning meeting, they decided to take on the following tasks from the Product Backlog:

o Add "search the catalog" for customers to find products to add to their online shopping carts.

o Provide valuable product suggestions to repeat customers.

o Update and expand the payment platform.

If the team finds that the velocity and capacity doesn't fit the selected items, an item could be switched to match these. Fortunately, in our example, the Pineapples Inc. team has done a great job picking the tasks so they don't need to be switched out. Thus, based on these tasks, the sprint goal should be formulated. Now, this may sound like a chore, since the items mentioned above seem diverse. However, the Product Owner didn't prioritize these for no reason. She/he most likely values the aggregate contribution of these three items and has an image of the product in mind when receiving an increment combining these backlog items. The sprint goal could be: "Develop a self-service, transactional solution that allows Pineapples Inc. shoppers to buy goods and receive product suggestions."

When you create the Sprint Backlog, the Product Owner and Development Team will gather in the same room. The Product Owner will then present the backlog items that they will take on, answer any issues, and then the team will discuss the design. For example, let's take the first Product Backlog item mentioned above. This is all about "searching the catalog." This backlog item can be divided into smaller tasks, such as creating the actual page where customers can search, writing the code and queries, and testing the search function. After the tasks are defined, place the expected amount of time each task will take. For example, creating the page will take seven hours, writing the code and queries will take another ten hours, and testing everything costs eleven hours. All elements needed to complete the backlog item should be reduced to tasks like these that can be taken on day in, day out. Of course, the hours spent can vary and can change as time progresses. But don't worry. Eventually, the team gets smarter and more accurate at assigning times to specific tasks.

Successful Scrum teams tend to use a primary method when creating these smaller tasks, or Sprint Backlog items. With ample focus, they strive toward tackling these items even if they seem challenging. Everything the Scrum team does—every decision they make and action they take—is done with an acronym in mind, namely: SMART. Intense concentration on fulfilling the elements of this acronym is what enables excellent Scrum teams to accomplish what other teams would only see in their dreams. According to a study from Willis Towers Watson, half of all managers do not set practical employee goals, let alone goals for Sprint Backlog items. So, what does SMART even mean, and how can it help the Scrum team?

SMART is a way to check whether objectives are **S**pecific, **M**easurable, **A**cceptable, **R**ealistic, and **T**ime-bound. Goals are often formulated vaguely. They seem more like wishes than concrete goals. To finish a sprint in the stipulated time, I highly advise you use SMART.

Specific. Being specific means that it is clear to everyone what the objective is and what result you want to achieve. To make a goal specific, ask these questions:

- What do we want to achieve?
- Why do we want to achieve it?
- When does it happen?
- Who is involved?
- Where will it happen?

In brief, describe the goal clearly and concretely, with a perceptible action, behavior, or result to which a number, amount, percentage, or other quantitative data is attached.

Measurable. This relates to the quality of the efforts to be made. How much are we going to do? How can we measure that? What is the result when we are finished? You must be able to see, hear, taste, smell, or feel a SMART goal. There must be a system, method, and procedure to determine the extent to which the goal has been achieved at a given moment. If possible, conduct a baseline assessment to determine the starting point.

Acceptable. If you set a SMART goal for yourself, it is enough that you accept it yourself. However, when you set a goal for a group of people, there must be support and the team members must agree with it. Otherwise, they will not take the necessary responsibility to achieve the goal. When individual objectives and organizational objectives are not aligned, the goal will not be delivered, or the change will not last. There are various methods to make sure goals are well-aligned. The primary way is to make sure there is engagement between you and your team members. You have to actively involve your team members in choosing and formulating the objectives. Every team member must have an opportunity to give her/his word.

Furthermore, some experts tend to explain "A" as: "Action-oriented" or "Achievable." These terms indicate necessary elements for a successful goal, namely, they show us that a goal needs to provoke action and be something the team can achieve. Keep in mind that a goal formulated the SMART-way prescribes a particular result, not an effort.

Realistic. Is the goal achievable? Is there a feasible plan requiring acceptable effort? Can the parties involved influence the requested results? Do they have sufficient know-how, capacity, resources, and capabilities? It is essential to take a closer look at these aspects because an unattainable goal does not motivate people. Sometimes the "R" in SMART is also explained as "Relevant." A feasible and meaningful goal is motivating. A realistic objective takes practice into account. There is no organization where people work on one goal for one hundred percent of the time. There are always other activities, unexpected events, and distractions.

An objective can also be unrealistic if it is imposed on the organization at a level that is too low. For instance, the goal: "Increase profits by nine percent in one year," is not a good target for the marketing department, because profit is an integral result of the entire company. A goal that is too easy to achieve is not exciting either, because it does not challenge the Scrum team. It is best to set goals that are just above the level of the team so that they keep improving. If people feel that they have to go the extra mile to hit a goal, they'll feel much better when they achieve it. This fosters energy for further goals in different sprints.

Time-bound. In general, SMART is used for more short-term goals. Thus, it's perfect for making more sense of the Sprint Backlog items, because these are carried out daily. Take into account that it is essential to know that a SMART objective has a definite start and end date. The following questions can help you further:

- o When will we be ready?
- o When do we start the activities?
- o When has the goal been achieved?

To further illustrate a well-defined and not-so-well-defined SMART-goal, check this out:

- o Well-defined: "At the end of sprint one, on Monday the second of December, the team wants a finished search page with features X, Y, and Z, where customers can search the catalog to find products to add to the online shopping cart."

- o Not-so-well-defined: "As a team, we want a nice search page for customers." This goal is not specific enough, not measurable, not acceptable, not realistic (because you don't know what to do), and not time-bound.

When the goals are set, make sure everyone commits verbally to the goals or Sprint Backlog items.

We've previously mentioned sprints, but let's zoom in to know what the Sprint event is all about. In most cases, the sprint is time-boxed to a couple of weeks, anywhere from two-to-four weeks and nothing more. Don't waver from this unless there is a great reason to do so.

As you know, setting goals is crucial for any success. The same goes for a successful sprint. Therefore, make sure every sprint you run has an understandably stated sprint goal, visible for anyone on the Development Team and any stakeholder. After each sprint, you should have a releasable increment of the product. For example, a login screen and the ability for users to log in to the platform of an e-learning company. Though the login screen may be done, this doesn't mean you deliver this incremental product to the market. But it should have the potential to go to production with as little effort as possible. Finally, the scope is set by the Scrum Team and not the sales or marketing department.

Stand-up Meeting: Execution

Another event is the Daily Scrum or stand-up meeting. This event is time-boxed at not more than fifteen minutes. With a Scrum team of around five-to-nine members and a concise Sprint Backlog, this is long enough. Beware of exceeding this stipulated time. The stand-up meeting is not the time for intricate details in terms of design or development. You can have other meetings to do that. Specifically, with this event, you get to know what work every team member did yesterday, what they will do today, and if they have encountered any obstacles along the way. During the stand-up meeting, each member of the Scrum team answers the following questions:

- What have I achieved since the last stand-up meeting?

- What am I going to achieve today?

- Do I expect obstacles, and can the team help me in some way?

Some people may "answer" the questions without answering them, so it is important to be clear and give context. In my experience, I have heard various professionals answer these questions, but many other team members were still oblivious to what they were doing.

There are many ways to conduct stand-up meetings; some may be more constructive than others. Holding the daily scrum or stand-up meeting is something you do every working day. The stand-up meeting is primarily for the Development Team. The Scrum Master should be there as much as she/he can to make sure everything is going well. If there are other stakeholders available, they can come, but they should keep any questions until after the meeting. Make sure you make a place for the stand-up meeting; keep the same time and place for this meeting.

To make things clearer, fill your physical Scrum board or digital Scrum board. This Scrum board gives the team a visual representation of the work. The team members will still answer the questions, but it now becomes more visible. Thus, even if you, as a team member, might not be working on a task, you can see the tasks that aren't done yet and if anything is blocking a task from being performed.

An example of a Scrum board is the following: a white board divided into five sections with Post-it Notes attached to each section. The first section is called "PB Items." this is all about the Product Backlog items you choose in this specific sprint. Again, this can be anything from user stories, all the way to bugs. Usually, user stories or bugs are grouped to take care of them in one sprint. However, sometimes, this is not possible due to a pressing bug that must be fixed as soon as possible. Thus, you'll end up with a few user stories and a bug to fix in the first section of "PB Items."

Afterward, jot down each task on a Post-it Note and place it on the Scrum board. The second section, "Not Done" indicates the tasks that are not yet completed. This is where all the tasks start. When someone from the Development Team takes on a task she/he moves the Post-it to the third section, "In Progress." This section contains all Post-it Notes for tasks that people are still working on. Afterward, in the fourth section, "Done," we place all the tasks that are finished. If all tasks relating to a specific user story have been finished, for example, we then put that user story in this section as well. During the sprint, some impediments may occur. Therefore, the fifth section is designated to deal with obstacles the team may encounter. This way, the Scrum Master can quickly see the barriers blocking the team from moving forward, and figure out a solution, so that the team can continue with the tasks for that particular backlog item.

It is too bad that in practice, we see that a lot of impediments are not tackled. The Scrum Master should bring these forth and get rid of them. This is especially the case if the same obstacles pop up for several days. Even if it is the Scrum Master that solves the obstacles, the team should make them clear, because they are working on the tasks where barriers occur. To give the team a better perspective on the tasks and time they take, we make a burndown chart. The burndown chart provides the visual information needed to manage your project or Scrum sprint daily. The graph shows the remaining amount of work left for the total project or the current sprint. This progress is made clear with the help of two lines:

- Line 1: Remaining work.
- Line 2: Ideal situation.

The sum of all the points on the Product Backlog is the total amount of "work." In other words: the whole estimated "size" of your project. You make the progress of the project evident by continually comparing the number of delivered story points to the elapsed time, marking this on the burndown chart. Most of the time, this is done to cover the number of weeks a sprint has.

Sprint Review and Sprint Retrospective

Finally, we'll take a look at the sprint review and sprint retrospective. The sprint review is when the Scrum team shows the work done in the sprint to the stakeholders, to collect feedback. This meeting is also referred to as "the demo," but the sprint review isn't just about that. Primarily, it is about the feedback and what you do with it. The sprint review takes a maximum of two hours for sprints of two weeks. The sprint review is a meeting where mutual understanding is cultivated, because it is never the case that you can describe exactly what you need in a product well in advance. Besides, most desires and wishes change during product development, and traditionally more features are required than what was initially thought.

Therefore, it is important to get as much feedback as possible for every sprint.

It is costly to make something and only hear about the changes needed very late in the process. In Scrum, we do things differently, because we know that the customer changes her/his mind constantly. Scrum gives a lot of freedom, but this only works with a lot of discipline, hard work, and communication.

In this meeting, the team gives a demo of the completed work. That is often a demo of the application, but that can also be other things. If the product increment isn't done, doing a demo is not a very smart thing to do, but it is important to mention why things aren't completed. For instance, if the application does not have a user interface yet, the team can also show test results and documentation. An All-Star Scrum Team can do a demo at any time in the sprint. Always try to get under the skin of the stakeholder and try to make the demo as interactive as possible. Do not show results that do not meet the team's definition of done. You want to entice the stakeholders to push the Product Owner for a release at the end of the sprint. If things are correct, you could receive questions like: "Why don't we put this into production?" It would be painful to admit that the product is not ready because the definition of done contains an error, like something that can't be accomplished in this given sprint.

The sprint retrospective is all about the Scrum team inspecting, adapting, and looking back at the sprint. Here we talk about the positives and negatives. What elements or tasks went well? What items or tasks didn't go well? What can we do better in the next sprints? This is the event where the Scrum team should learn multiple lessons. These can be jotted down in a plan to improve after each sprint. This continuous improvement is what sets Scrum apart from other methodologies. A good sprint retrospective stands or falls with its atmosphere. Ideally, it should have an atmosphere in which team members feel at ease and that they are safe to give and receive constructive criticism and discuss errors. If the team can't do that, it becomes challenging to find improvements, and the observations remain superficial. That is why it is especially visible in a sprint retrospective if a Scrum Master is also the manager—or behaves accordingly. A team that feels assessed by the Scrum Master, whether that is literal or not, is less likely to speak up.

Many elements can be named for creating a winning environment, such as making evident that the meeting is for the improvement of the entire Development Team. It is an excellent opportunity to stand still and look back at the sprint, to come up with some worthwhile improvements. Usually, the Scrum Master facilitates this meeting. It is precisely the way of Scrum to challenge yourself to become better continually, and that is why this is often one of the most important meetings for the Scrum Master. Not only to facilitate it, but also to challenge the team to always keep improving themselves not only as professionals, but also as people. Furthermore, the Product Owner could join this meeting as well. If the Development Team doesn't feel this is the right thing, the retrospective can be divided into two parts; one with the Product Owner and one without.

After the meeting, the release plan can be reviewed and updated based on the empirical data, such as elicited feedback from stakeholders. When the sprint retrospective is finished, the entire process is repeated by starting from the beginning, i.e., with the Product Backlog and the sprint planning sessions. In the coming chapter, we'll delve deeper into how all these things tie together!

Chapter 7: Breaking Down a Scrum Project

In the previous chapters, we learned more about Scrum and its roles, artifacts, ceremonies, and more critical concepts. But how are all these matters implemented in your organization? What does Scrum look like in practice? These and many more questions will be addressed in this chapter. I'll give you insights into how you can assemble the Scrum team, create your Product Backlog, user stories, prioritizing items, estimation, the release plan, and how all these are supported by "Sprint Zero" and a product vision.

Sprint Zero and Product Vision

When the team wants to embark on their project journey, usually, there is a lot to "fix" before the team is ready to go. Just think about crafting your product vision, setting up the initial Product Backlog, and filling and prioritizing the backlog with tasks for at least two sprints. We take two sprints because this keeps the Product Backlog concise enough, but also leaves room to take on additional tasks when there is room for it. Although you might wish to start straight away, you should take care of these things first. A way to "begin" the project straight away and still prepare what is needed, we introduce

Sprint Zero. This is the sprint where we set everything up, tidy up things, and make the team ready to fly. Thus, sprint zero is also great for crafting your initial release plan. And don't worry about not having sufficient empirical evidence to start crafting this plan or the backlog. Just make sure something is in place and understand that all artifacts are dynamic. Furthermore, this is the sprint to create an environment for success. Besides getting your team members focused on the sprint goal, having an environment that favors continuous integration will come in handy.

For instance, if a software company were to start sprint zero, they would create or set up a place where the coding rules are clarified; where the programmers have to write the code; where the code is tested; and where it can be deployed. Having such an environment in place allows for seamless and quick processes during the entire sprint. With each sprint, we aim to deploy something useful as soon as possible. Don't get me wrong; this "something" doesn't have to be unusual or perfect, ready for a customer to delve into. Nope, not at all. But it should be something you can move forward with and which complements other product increments later down the road. Undertaking a "Sprint Zero" is not imperative for your Scrum project, but it can help you set things up before you and your team get to the nitty-gritty work of creating the product. Make sure you set a clear deadline, which for a sprint is usually between two-to-four weeks. After this time, move on. Don't get stuck in this phase.

Crafting the product vision will give you perspective on the product, especially what it is and what value it brings to whom. Usually, you are building a product for a target audience. And often, you are not part of this target audience yourself. Therefore, don't just "think" of what the customer might like, ask them instead. The team has to be clear who the product is for, who the target audience is, and what to deliver based on the data gathered from the target audience. To illustrate this further, let's say you are leading a project for a home security company. The company wants to develop a new security system easily employed by the elderly.

Before conducting the whole project, some staff from the security company should have spoken with the target audience and gained solicited opinions, feedback, and insights. These can then be discussed with the Scrum team before it creates in the product vision. Remember, this is not the time to get into various details. The product vision is dynamic too, but everyone in the team should at least know the target audience and purpose of doing the project. Below I'll list some qualities for crafting an awesome product vision:

Make it broad and inspiring. It is impossible to be specific in the beginning phases of any project. This is what makes the waterfall method so sloppy. People try to predict how everything in the project may unfold. This is simply impossible. There are always multiple variables that change. So, make the product vision broad but inspiring, so that people have a general idea of what they are trying to achieve and why. Make the "why" very clear and robust, and you will win.

Clear and stable. Although employing various buzzwords seems to be a trend nowadays, don't fool yourself into thinking this should be the case for the product vision. Avoid complicated, unnecessarily long, and tedious language. Instead, be different, and make it clear and easily consumable for all team members, be they experienced or just starting in their role. Also, the specific vision should not be changed too often, if at all. It is better to keep it stable to avoid confusion among team members.

Short and sweet. In the failing waterfall method, we see that professionals with high salaries make documents that are countless pages long. And what do you think the problem is with all of this? Well, let me tell you; the biggest problem is that no one reads all these documents. They are too long, complicated, and hidden from the crowd. Usually, after creating these documents, they end up somewhere in a drawer collecting dust. So, keep the product vision as short as possible. Why not do it on only one page that you can print out for others to see?

To keep these qualities fresh and the product vision in mind, you can discuss it during sprint reviews. Besides, I would like to share an example of how an inspiring product vision can come about. There was a CEO of a medical software and hardware company that helped craft the product vision in projects. Before crafting any plan, he would begin with a powerful speech about his son, who was very sick at birth. Due to his son's sickness, the CEO was often present at the hospital, where he was surprised to find many processes were very inefficient, ineffective, and slow. This fueled him to build his company to make the processes in hospitals quicker, more effective, and efficient to help more people in less time. This makes for a very inspiring message that pretty much any reasonable human being can relate to. Also, the product vision was placed on a single page and stuck on a wall near the Scrum team. Thus, it was always clear who the team was serving and how they were serving them.

The Initial Product Backlog

As explained earlier, the Product Backlog contains all the requirements of the product. Basically, it includes all items that you and your team should take care of to deliver the product and create value for the customer and organization. Its dynamic nature lends itself to the ever-changing markets, technology, and customer desires. The most valuable items are always on the top. These should be taken care of before anything else. The Product Owner has placed these items at the top for a reason, so get to work on these first and tackle them as quickly and efficiently as possible. The Product Backlog is prioritized by value, and it is more detailed on the top and less at the bottom. Eventually, you will get more detail when items move to the top. Although the Product Owner manages and prioritizes all backlog items, it's the Development Team that estimates the tasks, because they are the ones doing the work.

Generally, your Product Backlog contains user requirements, new features or enhancements and their descriptions, and technical requirements when things in the infrastructure need to change. These types of technical requirements aren't directly related to the customer. Make sure you limit them as much as you can. This doesn't mean that you should overlook them, not at all. Take them into account, but don't ever think they are the main reason why the work needs to be done. Always keep yourself and the team focused on the product vision. Without doing so, the team ends up forgetting this end goal due to the day-to-day work they are performing. Always find time to reflect and briefly look at the big picture. The same goes for bugs in the current system that block further development of the incremental product. You need to limit the bugs to remain focused on what the user or customer sees as value. I have said this multiple times already, but it's vital to reiterate: be certain that the Product Backlog is the *only* source of everything that needs to be done for the product. It includes everything from user and technical requirements, all the way to the various bugs that need to be fixed. So, there is no room for extra documents or places to jot down issues. This makes the whole process significantly more transparent. Transparency is important for any worthwhile project.

After filling the Product Backlog, the next step is prioritizing and estimating all backlog items. The key element in prioritizing anything is to make sure the item with the most value is at the top. In this context, with the value, we mean business value, namely the monetary aspect of things: increasing revenue. Another critical element is to group requirements wherever you see fit. Usually, various requirements or user stories are too big to tackle in a single sprint. Thus, you are better off splitting them. Less frequently, you might find similar or smaller requirements. Check if they can be bundled together and can be tackled in a sprint. Finally, I highly advise you to assign a business value metric to each story. Follow these steps carefully:

Jot down all your user stories on Post-it Notes.

Place the Post-it Notes on a wall or whiteboard. Just stick them right on the wall without thinking about any order.

Now, you have ten "value" points to spend on each user story. Which user story gets the most points? When you can answer this question, place that user story on top, followed by the next user story with the highest score.

If you are working in a larger organization or with a ton of user stories, ten "value" points may not be enough. Thus, you can take a broader range, such as 500 points or even 1000 points. The point is that you end up with a clearly prioritized Product Backlog based on the business value.

Tackling the most valuable item on the backlog might not be something that is needed in the initial stages of the software. In traditional project methodologies, you have no option but to develop all elements of the initial phase before moving on. Fortunately, with Scrum, you can develop the product increment with the most value first, be it something belonging to the initial phase of any other phase.

User Stories

User stories are necessary for gathering user requirements. This helps to form the requirements. A user story is short and simple; a watered-down requirement. Don't make them too detailed. Make sure they are made from the user's perspective. Usually, the developers are not the ones interacting with the product, so make sure the results or requirements for the users are formulated correctly. User stories make it easy to discuss the product, so focus on this. There is a general format to a user story, namely: As a

<insert role> I want a <feature> so that <benefit>. Let's fill it in: "As an online clothes shopper I want to be able to search the website catalog so that I can find clothes to purchase." In this example, we used the role of "online clothes shopper," however, most websites are used by various people. So, for this example, you could also have a user who is a "discount clothes shopper." Based on the role, variables can be improved and innovated to match the specific user's desires. To do so properly, make a persona for each of the different types of users interacting with the website. A persona is a fictional representation of a specific user, such as "Bob TheDiscountShopper." Afterward, you can fill their persona by writing about their age, gender, motivations, goals, personality, and more characteristics that seem necessary.

Often, user stories are written on cards. You can put the user stories on the wall or whiteboard, but for larger organizations, they should be available digitally as well. Related to this are the "conditions of satisfaction," which have the following qualities: they are required for acceptance; represent tests; and are specific. Detailed items can be addressed later, but first, the specifics or foundations need to be in place. It doesn't change the significance of the effort when something can be addressed at a later time, such as the color of a button.

For instance, for the previously mentioned user story about the "online clothes shopper" searching the website, we can name various conditions of satisfaction. Think of things such as: match against item title; category; description; and keywords. Another requirement could be advanced search techniques like quotes. Furthermore, something like "Results should return in less than three seconds," is an example of a condition that you'll see in practice.

The conditions can be placed on the back of the user stories as steps on how to demo the user story or increment product. For example: "Open search page, enter various keywords, initiate search," et cetera. There are qualities of good user stories found in the acronym INVEST:

o **Independent.** When organizations are starting with the implementation of Scrum, they tend to craft user stories that depend on other user stories. Beware that you don't make this mistake and double-check that the user story can be fulfilled without the need for another user story.

o **Negotiable.** Dealing with user stories helps us deal with discussions. By discussing elements of the user stories, we can negotiate how to further the user story, if something is missing or if elements are superfluous.

o **Valuable.** Every user story should contain something of value for the customer, organization, or both. If this isn't the case, the user story is wrong and needs correction. If the user story contains no clear-cut benefit, it is difficult to prioritize it, compared to other stories.

o **Estimate.** The team gives an estimation of the amount of work and time needed per user story.

o **Small.** Make sure multiple stories can be completed in a single sprint. You do this by keeping the user stories small.

o **Testable.** The conditions of satisfaction aren't only documented and then put away. Nope, they're also tested. When the Scrum team has done an excellent job formulating the conditions of satisfaction linked to a user story, it is easy for testers to check that the resulting features are working exactly the way the user needs.

It can sometimes be difficult to manage ideas in an organization. Ideas seem to appear from all branches and all kinds of professionals. Usually, these ideas can be used to formulate user stories, but an idea on its own is not enough. Frequently, ideas can be combined, added to, or reduced in ways that are useful for the project. Dealing with all these ideas can be a hurdle, but Scrum makes it simpler. Scrum teaches us the hierarchy to better categorize them. The hierarchy is:

- **Theme.** At the top of the hierarchy we find the theme. The theme is the overarching subject we focus on during an entire product release and sometimes even various releases. A theme is large and could never be put into multiple sprints, let alone a single sprint. Thus, it needs to be refined and reduced in size.

- **Epic.** This is the name for user stories that don't fit into a single sprint. The epic user stories could be achieved in various sprints, but they need to be broken down to take care of finishing them in parts, one step (or sprint) at a time.

- **User story.** Finally, we reach something that can be finished in a single sprint, the user story. Generally, in my experience, we always solved multiple user stories in a sprint, at least two. If this seems impossible for your team, make sure there is a way to split your user stories even further. Most of the time, it will be possible to do this.

Thus, before the Product Backlog is filled, make sure there is no way to reduce the size of the user story. Remember that it is better to have a smaller user story, easily achieved in a sprint, than a user story that could easily take up two, three, or even four sprints! During the sprints, always remember that developing goes iteratively and that you release the work incrementally. Sprint after sprint, we aim to develop or solve parts of a big puzzle. The process of developing parts of the puzzle is iterative. When a more substantial part of the puzzle is completed, such as the entire top section, we release this. Numerous sprints later, we release the middle section and bottom section. This process is incremental and is done until the puzzle is completed.

Crafting the Release Plan

Now that the Product Backlog is prioritized and estimated and the All-Star Scrum team is ready to go, we are prepared to create the release plan. When crafting the release plan, think of the term "velocity." Velocity within Scrum is a measurement of the amount of work the Scrum team can finish each sprint. Put differently, it is all about the answer to the question: "How many of these backlog items can we do in one sprint?" Take a look at the image below.

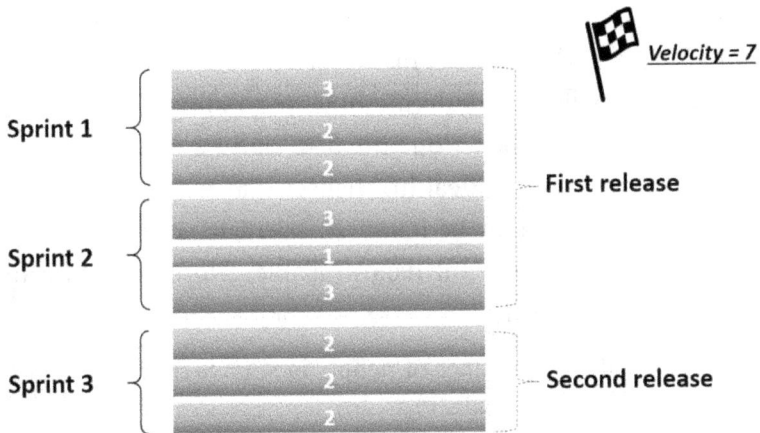

Don't worry if the image seems overwhelming. It isn't as complicated as it may look. Let me explain. In this image, the Scrum team is using a velocity of seven. This means that no more than seven story points can be taken up for each sprint. The velocity of seven is based on previous experience with the Scrum team. If your team is completely new to Scrum, start off with a lower velocity of five, to get a feeling of how the method works. In this example, the velocity is seven, and as you see, in sprint one the total amount of items that we take on is seven (3+2+2 = 7). The same goes for sprint two (3 + 1 + 3 = 7). However, in sprint three we see something different, the number is six (2 + 2 + 2 = 6). Why? Because if we take the "one" from sprint two and change it with the "two" from sprint three we would end up with "eight," thus exceeding the velocity. So, plan based on the experiences of previous projects. After the sprints are divided, the team can figure out when something can be released. In this example, two releases are marked: one at the end of sprint two and one at the end of sprint three. Thus, the team and stakeholders know when they can expect to release a product increment. Often, the Scrum team has a strict deadline before a release. This deadline might be set after sprint one, for instance. By discussing the current progress, stakeholders can point out if certain story points need to be in the next release. Then the team can adapt and move these story points to the top to take care of them earlier. But beware, make sure the velocity is not exceeded. You might still be wondering how to go about figuring out your team's velocity when you are just starting with Scrum. Well, although it is not ideal to figure out your velocity without empirical data, it may be handy to calculate your initial velocity if there isn't any empirical data available. Here is the formula to calculate the velocity:

- Take the number of people in your Scrum team; let's say we have **six** professionals (P).
- Afterward, count the number of sprints and weeks of each sprint, let's say we have three sprints of **2** weeks each (S).
- Now, count the days the team is available to work on these sprints, for this example, **39** (D).
- Take a factor of $\frac{1}{4}$.
- Fill in the formula $P^2 + S^2 + D^2 \div \frac{1}{4} = V^2$

I hope you figured out that this is absolutely ludicrous and not at all possible! Although many people think figuring out these metrics is quickly done by filling out a formula, they are far from right. For a beginning Scrum team, there are immense amounts of variables you have to take into consideration. No formula on earth can fix that for you, except for trying, failing, repairing, and doing it again. So, instead of filling in this silly formula, have a discussion with your newly formed Scrum team about the backlog. Give each team member her/his say in terms of the various backlog items and how long they think the items will take. Then let all team members discuss the options and allow them to identify how many backlog items they can get done, for example: the top three items on the backlog. Then add up the number of story points of these three items, let's say the amount is nine. Then take that amount as your initial velocity for the first sprint. There is a high probability it is still wrong. But hey, we now at least have some empirical data we can learn from and do better next sprint. Right? During your Scrum project journey, more data will be gathered. After a couple of sprints, you can quickly figure out the velocity for best-case scenarios and for worst-case scenarios. When an item is very pressing and needs to get done, you can look at the velocity for the worst-case scenario (the worst the team has ever done), so that the team is confident they can get it done.

Chapter 8: Understanding Scrum Metrics

Scrum metrics are instruments for measuring the Scrum process. But what can you precisely measure? Well, you can measure a lot. Think about things like the development process; quality of work; productivity; predictability; and the products being developed. Scrum metrics focus on the value that is delivered to the customer. Besides Scrum metrics, there are also other agile metrics you should know about, namely:

• Kanban metrics: focus on the workflow, organizing and prioritizing work to complete this. A widely used metric is cumulative flow.

• Lean metrics: focus on valuation metrics from the entire organization to the customer and eliminating "waste." Popular metrics are lead time and cycle time.

But the metrics we address in this chapter are Scrum metrics, which focus on the predictability of a working product (or product increment) for customers. Commonly used metrics are team velocity and the burndown chart. We should care about these metrics, because by measuring you gain valuable insights into multiple Sprints, versions, when bugs are discovered, and more.

There are various elements that make metrics useful. Without these elements it is difficult to garner benefits from them. Consider the following:

• **Ensure that you use metrics that result in meaningful conversations.** For instance, after crafting the burndown chart, the team members can come together and discuss the current trajectory from time to time. Thus, they can figure out if meaningful progress is made.

• **The benefit of metrics is that you make the whole process more empirical.** Scrum relies on empirical data to a large degree. Thus, if you have metrics that support the gathering of this data, you support the whole Scrum process too. Think of data such as the speed at which a particular test can be performed.

• **Check if metrics can be combined.** Sometimes it is useful to combine various metrics to get a clearer image of the Development Team's progress. Think of metrics like productivity (e.g., the number of tasks completed in a specific time) and velocity.

• **Ensure that the entire team comes up with the metrics.** The Development Team has a say concerning selecting the metrics. The Scrum Master and Product Owner also have a say. They can proffer Key Performance Indicators (KPI's) or metrics, like velocity.

• **Don't complicate things!** When you pick metrics, make them quickly understood. Also, calculating them shouldn't involve any advanced math.

Burndown and Burn-up Charts

You now might have the question, "How can I make a burndown chart?" To start measuring the team's progress. Well, that is pretty simple, by following these steps:

1. Draw a y-axis and an x-axis on a flip chart, whiteboard, or using any software.

2. Plot the story points or "work" on the y-axis. This is the sum of task-estimates in, for example, days.

3. Plot the time on the x-axis and include the total duration of your sprint or project. This is the iteration timeline, usually in days.

4. During your project, you measure from $t = 0$ at fixed intervals how much "work" has been delivered. In a sprint that takes fifteen days, you can measure at intervals of three days, for instance.

5. What remains is some basic math, namely working out the: Total – Delivered. Not very advanced for most people, I hope.

6. Now is the time to plot the result of this calculation in the graph. The points marked out for "Actual Tasks Remaining" should result in a downward line. The line shows per point how much "work" remains of the total you started with.

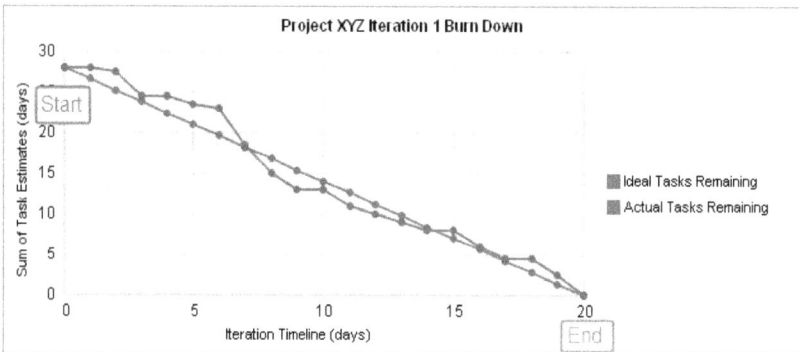

The descending "Actual Tasks Remaining" line follows the measurement points that you plot yourself in the graph. The "ideal" line in a burndown runs diagonally from the top left corner to the bottom right corner. The "ideal line" indicates precisely the average number of points that must be "delivered" per day to reach the project or sprint goal in the set time. When reading the graph, use the "ideal line" as follows:

- The distance between the real line (below or above) and the ideal line indicates how much the project is ahead or behind in the planning.
  - If the actual line is above the ideal line, the project is running behind schedule.
  - If the actual line is below the ideal line, the project is ahead of schedule.

Besides the burndown charts, you and your team can also decide to work with "burn-up" charts. The main difference between the two is that instead of tracking how many tasks are remaining, we track how many tasks or how much "work" we have finished. Doing so makes the curve go up instead of down. A burn-up chart comes in handy when the scope decreases or when the team happens to complete some work and shortly after finds that there is more work to get through for a new client, for instance. A burn-up chart makes these events more evident because progress is tracked independently based on how the scope of work changes or how the sum of task-estimates—or the "work" to be done—changes. In a burndown chart, there is no room to change the x-axis. With a burn-up chart, this is possible, because the "desired line" of ideal tasks remaining is a horizontal line that can change around. Take these steps to make a burn-up chart:

1. You plot the story points or "work" on the y-axis.
2. You plot the time on the x-axis and include the total duration of your sprint or project.
3. During your project, you plot the total amount of story points or "work" in the graph from $t = 0$ at fixed intervals.
4. At the same intervals, you measure how much "work" has been done, and you also plot this in the graph.
5. This then results in two lines: the relatively horizontal "total amount of work" line and the ascending "completed work" line. A burn-up chart clearly shows the completed "work" relating to the total amount of "work" in your project. The project is complete when the lines intersect.

This is how you make a burn-up chart. You can use any method you would like to make it clear, such as drawing it out on a whiteboard or creating one in Excel. Now that we have a burn-up chart, we should use and read it properly. The Development Team should compare the amount of work that is completed against the total amount of work in the project every working day. The distance between the two lines is, therefore, the amount of work that remains. As said, the project is completed when the two lines meet, i.e., intersect. The "ideal line" indicates precisely the average number of points, i.e., tasks that must be delivered each day to reach the project or sprint goal in the stipulated time. When reading the graph, use the "ideal line" as follows:

> • The distance between the "completed work" line (below or above) and the ideal line indicates how much the project is ahead or behind on the schedule.
> • When the line for "completed work" is below the ideal line, the project is running behind schedule.
> • When the line for "completed work" is above the ideal line, the project is ahead of schedule.

Furthermore, the line that indicates the total amount of work makes evident when work has been added to or removed from the sprint. If "work" is added to the project or sprint, the distance between the two lines becomes greater. The influence on the planned end date is, therefore, clear. To make this clear, you draw a trend line that is based on the average amount of points that are delivered by the team. The new end date of your project is where this trend line crosses the (increased) total work line.
You can experiment with both burndown charts and burn-up charts. Mainly if the Development Team includes members who are new to Scrum, this is important. Besides experimenting with both methods to see what fits well with the team, some projects demand a particular approach. There are projects which revolve more around one of these two questions:

1. Do you want to monitor the progress of your sprint in detail and share it with customers and stakeholders regularly?

2. Do you want to make progress visible in the simplest way for the team and those directly involved?

A burn-up chart shows the completed work and the total project size in one overview. In contrast to the burndown chart that only shows the remaining work with one line. Because the total project size with the burn-up chart is clear, you get answers to questions such as: has too much new "work" been added?

This information is useful for identifying and resolving problems within the sprint, e.g., a customer who is constantly changing the scope, putting the end-result at risk. Use the burn-up chart for reasons such as:

- **You want to show regular updates on how the sprint is progressing.** If you regularly present the project progress to the same audience, for example, weekly progress meetings for customers, use the burn-up chart. This makes it easy to see the progress, including the additional work and the consequences it brings forth.

- **If the scope has a "dynamic" character.** When "work" is suddenly added to the sprint, a burn-up chart is more valuable. In some projects, the customer can be very pressing and ask for additional functionality. Besides, some tasks could be removed if they are not necessary anymore. Usually, the latter is caused by unexpected problems with costs, budget, and time. In a project where customers add or remove a lot of work during the project, a burndown chart is not a complete representation of the progress.

- **When the scope expands.** When the project scope is gradually expanded, sometimes far beyond the original framework, a burn-up chart is more useful. With a burndown chart, it would appear as if little progress has been made by the team, which is not necessarily the case, i.e., the scope could have been expanded. Thus, a burn-up makes the issue at hand much clearer for the customer. This makes the issue discussable and allows for a quick adjustment whenever necessary.

Why should you use a burndown chart instead? There are a few reasons:

- **Very easy to employ.** Burndown charts are easy to make and follow up. They have an obvious line to show when the project or sprint is finished. Starting with a burndown chart is particularly advisable for new Development Teams. Why? Because, every team member will understand the graph with little to no explanation. Thus, making a burndown chart for presentations is desirable for customers or stakeholders from a non-technical background. However, don't forget that the burndown chart does leave out some crucial information. It doesn't tell the whole story of the sprint. So, for more complex sprints, with changes in the scope, this isn't very useful.

- **The scope has a "static" character.** Burndown charts are usually employed with projects where the project doesn't change at all. Projects or sprints with a fixed scope don't need the additional information of a burn-up chart. This would make the project unnecessarily more complex. Maybe it wouldn't even be more complex, but just not useful at all. When things are simple, keep them simple. Any unneeded variable you add to your plate makes the project exponentially more difficult.

- **Helps keep the momentum high.** The burndown chart can keep the team's momentum going and can motivate them to push through until the end of the sprint. When people are starting with Scrum, these quick wins build confidence. And confidence is the quality that the Development Team needs to deliver quality product increments. When the team members are all more confident, they create, provide, and bring more value to the customer.

Chapter 9: How to Excel and Common Mistakes

There are various ways to excel as a Scrum Master or Product Owner. Multiple ways have been addressed already, such as being transparent with your team members and being open to their opinions and feedback. In Scrum, you always strive to make the users or customers happy. Preferably with something tangible. Thus, when you are new to Scrum, don't take on a large and complex development job from the get-go. To excel, take a business project whereby the users don't care about all the intricacies of the product. For instance, if you are creating a marketing tool for the Marketing Department, they are less interested in how the programming code ties together and how well it is documented. They just want a working tool, that's it. Also, starting with a small project gives you more confidence. Ensure success first and scale up afterward. Start with one product, one Product Owner, one Scrum Master, and a team of five or six people. Don't think that you can convert the entire company in one day.

So, a short project is good to start with, but by short, I don't mean *very* short. A very short project probably gives you too little time to see Scrum work adequately. Then the success of the project depends more on some "heroic deeds" by some team members. Moreover, small projects are not sufficiently representative. If the project is a success, then you will still be told: "We would get the same results with the old method." I would say a project of about two to three months is fine to start using Scrum with.

A common mistake we notice is that new Scrum teams take on projects that aren't "real." In other words, a project whereby it doesn't matter if things go wrong. That is pretty much the worst thing you can do. An unimportant project receives no attention, and therefore no focus, no stakeholder involvement, and no worthwhile meetings. With an important project, it is much easier to get people motivated. And you don't have to be afraid that things will go wrong: as a team member you already have skills and are able to achieve goals, no matter which method you use. Always add Scrum elements that make you better, never make a mistake to think that Scrum is a goal in itself. It's not. Instead, think of it as a way to work smarter, not harder. The business side of your organization is sensitive to this.

Another mistake a lot of Scrum Masters and Product Owners make is that they don't garner support from all layers of the organization. If everyone is new to the Scrum scene, it is possible to hire an experienced Scrum Master to start things off and to make sure that everyone supports the Scrum initiative. It is an experiment worth trying. Make sure that the Product Owner and the team members have a good reason to make it a personal success.

Also, don't be the one who is afraid of failing. You can never excel if you are allergic to failing. Instead, embrace the fact that failing is part of the process to gain the mastery you wish for. Then take the time to become better at Scrum and adhere to the rules of the game. Especially with a first Scrum adventure, there is a tendency to exaggerate. Think that every team goes through phases to become magnificent. This ties together with communication and transparency. Make sure you make all the problems visible. Scrum itself is not going to solve your problems, but it makes them readily available and puts them "right in your face." By gaining this visibility, you have the best chance that you can to mobilize people to solve the impediments.

Don't make the mistake of thinking that change happens overnight. I always show some character and a strong personality when needed. It is better to ask for forgiveness afterward than to ask for permission in advance. No room to discuss with stakeholders? Well, can you go outside and discuss it there? Are no users or customers visiting the demo? Find them and invite them for some coffee, and show what has been achieved. When you achieve anything meaningful during the implementation of Scrum, celebrate it! Give presentations, organize a dinner, or give a small gift to the team members and stakeholders. This will fire them up and help them in their growth.

Finally, another common mistake is completely forgetting the use of technology to facilitate the Scrum process. Nowadays, a myriad of Scrum tools exist which can set you up for success. Why not make use of these to keep the processes more streamlined? In the next chapter, various tools will be addressed that can fast-track your project's desired outcome.

Chapter 10: Scrum Software Tools for Workflow Management

In recent years, an enormous amount of software tools have found a place in the emerging technology market to ease the Scrum process. For a team that is not "co-located" and/or is not working full-time with Scrum, the benefits of a digital solution are crystal clear. Handy integrations with other digital platforms also add extra functionality and value. A physical project board still works best in terms of interaction, for example, during the stand-up meetings. And when creating transparency and insight into project status, a whiteboard filled with colorful Post-its is hard to beat.

From a functional point of view, the range of digital Scrum tools can be subdivided into: collaboration & documentation tools, such as Portals, where "knowledge" can be stored and shared; workflow managers, which are useful for managing workflows by using digital project boards; and messaging tools, to enable and streamline team communication. Also, it is possible to find tools that are a combination of these categories.

Some software companies specialize in one aspect, and others combine functionality. The advantage of an integrated solution is that everything "seamlessly" intertwines; a disadvantage of an integrated solution is that it sometimes contains a component that doesn't function well in the scheme of things. In the latter case, a combination of specific digital Scrum tools might have been a better solution. The prominent providers of integrated solutions compete with each other on functionality and price. Most tiers and price models are not far apart. The digital options often start with a free version with stripped-down functionality and a limited number of users. The first subsequent "Tier" (price level) will then be around $10 per user from fifteen users. From a functional point of view, the range of digital Scrum and agile tools is so extensive that it is difficult for the starting "Agilist" to make a choice, let alone the right choice. That is why we have given an overview here. This is, of course, not an exhaustive overview; the range of literally hundreds of applications is too broad for that.

We start with some entry-level tools that are completely free: Trello and Slack. If ease of use and progress reporting play an essential role from the start, Asana is a good choice for smaller organizations and teams. A more robust solution is advisable for larger organizations that want to implement Agile broadly. The Atlassian combination of Jira Core, Confluence, and Stride, offers a solution here. Take into account the fact that switching from your current application to a new application can be a great hassle. So, always make a very thoughtful decision and communicate things with the Scrum team. Here are the options to get yourself started:

> **Option 1: Use the free and simple tools Trello and Slack for small teams.** Trello is a workflow manager based on the Kanban board and has a free version with unlimited boards, lists, maps, members, checklists, and attachments. Trello is very easy to use and hardly has a learning curve. The instructional material is well put together and quickly

provides sufficient knowledge to be able to use the platform. The free version is highly recommended for starting Scrum teams. Slack is a Messaging tool and has a free version with an unlimited duration, but limited storage of 5GB and 10,000 messages. However, this is more than enough for small teams who want to try it out. The Slack Standard Plan costs around $7.25 per user per month.

Option 2: The Scrum tool Asana is great for larger teams, and when an organization wants to conduct multiple projects simultaneously. Asana is a widely used Scrum tool that combines a workflow and project manager with excellent team messaging and collaboration functionality. Asana has good reporting functions that provide insight into the progress of the various projects with a single click of the mouse. There is a free plan for up to fifteen users and a premium plan for around $9.99 per user per month.

Option 3: Scaling larger, more complex projects with enterprise-quality software by Atlassian. This comes with a combination of the following Atlassian products: Stride (a very comprehensive messaging tool); Confluence (a documentation and collaboration portal); and Jira Core (a workflow and project management application).

The team could also use things like G Suite by Google. Using G Suite by Google can help create Scrum artifacts and keep only one version of them. Thus, these documents can be updated in real-time, and team members can be invited to have read-only rights. This is important because the Product Backlog and other artifacts are very dynamic. During a project, things can change. Thus, requirements or backlog items in the Product Backlog can change too, and it might be useful for the team to have digital access to this information.

Conclusion

Due to technological advancements, there has been a shift in how we should tackle projects. New methods are needed to approach dynamic projects that are constantly shifting in scope. In this book, *Scrum: What You Need to Know About This Agile Methodology for Project Management,* we delved into the world of agile methodologies and specifically one of the most prominent in the category: Scrum. There is no doubt that using Scrum can skyrocket the success of your project to new heights. This book has demonstrated that it is indeed possible to do more with less.

In chapter one, we looked at project management methodologies of the past and present. We learned that traditional methods, such as the waterfall method, are far from ideal in today's dynamic world. This dynamism necessitates a method that allows for continuous improvement, iterative working, and rapid readjustments. An approach such as Scrum is the solution for today's project management problems.

The basics of Scrum were explained in chapter two. In chapter three we learned about Scrum's three crucial roles: Product Owner, Scrum Master, and the Development Team. They all work toward a common goal but have varying responsibilities. In chapter four, we took a closer look at how you can form a great Scrum team that delivers the results you wish for. Furthermore, in chapters five, six, and seven, we gave more detail about the Scrum artifacts, ceremonies, and how a Scrum project works in practice. Finally, we took a look at Scrum metrics, common mistakes, and some useful software to kick start your Scrum projects.

An iterative approach is used within Scrum to optimize predictability and to keep risks under control. You now know that three pillars are what sets it apart from other methodologies, namely: transparency, inspection, and adjustment/adaptation.

So, are you willing to embrace these agile concepts, values, and best practices to create and deliver more value for yourself, your organization, and your customers? What are you waiting for? Go and put things into practice and see for yourself what the Scrum method can help you and your team achieve!

Here's another book by Robert McCarthy
that you might be interested in

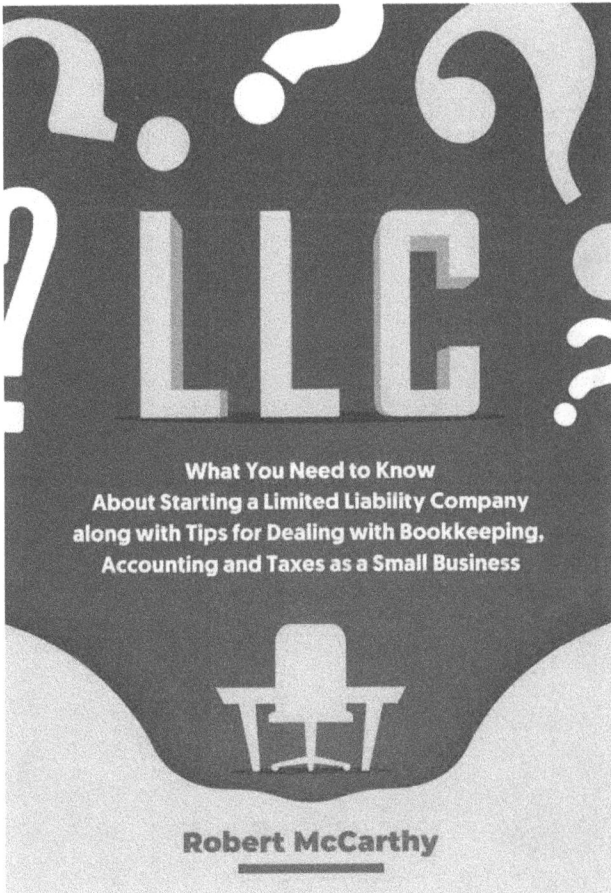

**What You Need to Know
About Starting a Limited Liability Company
along with Tips for Dealing with Bookkeeping,
Accounting and Taxes as a Small Business**

Robert McCarthy

www.ingramcontent.com/pod-product-compliance
Lightning Source LLC
Chambersburg PA
CBHW050640190326
41458CB00008B/2351